God With Us
Ortiz Missions Journey

by

Gamaliel and Cathi Ortiz

To Miguel, Kayla, Sandra, Isaac, & Aya

Remember God's Grace and Goodness

CONTENTS

PREFACE

We were missionaries to rural Haiti not one week ago. After spending six years in Haiti, our family chose to evacuate due to political unrest to the point that we believed not only were we in danger, but we were also a danger to our Haitian friends and colleagues by our continued presence in the country. In many ways we are still reeling from this abrupt exit. The following book is a narrative telling our story, including some of our blogs and newsletters from the mission field. But this isn't a story that is meant to be focused on us. It is a story of God's provision, protection, and power. Our prayer is that God himself stands out as the main character. On its own, while it may be a unique story, it is nothing special apart from him. It is God's grace manifested in our lives that makes this a story that needs to be retold. At the same time, it's a story of how God uses everyday people like you and us to do greater things outside of ourselves, because his grace is sufficient.

1 INTRODUCTION

This last Saturday I went to the barber shop to get a haircut. My brother-in-law, Mark, had said the previous day that he was going to get his hair cut and asked if I wanted to go. It had been almost a month since my last haircut and though Cathi would say I didn't need one, I felt I needed it. If for nothing else, at least I hoped it would give me the feeling of normalcy again. Walking out into the cold Michigan air in the middle of February was a stark contrast to the heat and humidity of Haiti. It would take a little time for my body to adjust to that difference. I almost chuckled to myself as we pulled out of the driveway, because even though it was gravel, it was so smooth compared to the dirt roads that I'd just spent the last week bouncing up and down on.

I sat down in the barber's chair and the sweet lady asked me how I was doing. I don't know that I've ever been so conflicted about that question before in my life.

"I'm alright, thanks," I think I managed to spit out before it got awkward.

"So what have you been up to?" she asked.

The first thought that came to my mind was that if I truthfully answered that question, there was no way she was going to believe me. At the beginning of the week I'd had rocks thrown at me. I had driven through barricades of burning tires in the middle of the road as armed gangsters threatened my life. How would I explain that I had taken a drive through hell three times this week and lived?

"You wouldn't believe me if I told you."

It seemed to at least satisfy her and she went on with my haircut. And while I sat there, I looked into the mirror in front of me, into the eyes of someone I almost didn't recognize. There were more wrinkles, for sure. But there was brokenness behind the eyes. I fought back tears as I looked back at myself. They were tears of sadness, yes. I had left a life that I'd known for six years in the most abrupt manner possible. I had seen things that I would not be able to erase from my memory that I'm sure will revisit me for some time to come. But they were also tears of gratitude. I had experienced and relied on God in ways I never had to before. He had guided me and comforted me as I led and cared for my family in the midst of turmoil. In my brokenness, God held me together in order that he might be glorified through this mess. The eyes that stared back at me also had a new perspective on the power, grace, and love of God. It's a story that begins long before I was dodging rocks and bullets in Haiti.

2 THE BEGINNING

After a highly emotional adolescence, I became very fact-driven; analytical and systematic; task-oriented, organized, highly stubborn with an ambitious nature, sworn to never make another emotional decision again. But God's timing was highly evident in the whole process. Ministry was not even on my radar. Granted, I served in the local church in lay positions with the youth as well as in leading worship. But full-time ministry was probably the furthest thing from my mind.

When I went to Trinity Christian College for my freshman year of college in the year 2000, I was trying to pick up the pieces of many wrong choices. I had graduated high school at 16 and run away from home - one of many emotionally-driven decisions. When I returned home it was only to enlist in the Marine Corps, which ended in a medical discharge for an old gymnastics injury. I was lost and searching. So, in August of 2000, I found myself in front of the choir room at Trinity, waiting for my audition to join the concert choir. In some way, going to a Christian school helped me feel like I was trying to make things right. I had gone to high school in Arlington Heights, a northwest suburb of Chicago and my parents now lived in a southwest suburb, not 30 minutes from Trinity. It was almost like an olive branch extended to my parents. It was a Christian school and it was close to home, so that I could be near my parents. Besides, I really liked the campus. It was a small school, removed from the hustle and bustle of downtown, yet close enough to enjoy day trips. It was close enough to home for me to commute and save money on tuition as well. On top of all that, they had a good music program. I had a knack for music and had taught myself to play the guitar, keyboard, and drums. I'd also just started experimenting with my voice and in writing music, so I wanted to explore it further.

Just in front of me in line for the audition was this beautiful girl with whom I struck up a conversation. Her curly hair, bronzed skin, and hazel eyes caught my attention, while her confidence held it. Her smile and her laugh completely disarmed me. She and I were both music majors and we hit it off well. We had the majority of our classes together because of the core music classes we needed to take. Because of our last names being so close together (Nelson and Ortiz), we were often paired up or next to each other in line ups - as was the case that day. We became good friends and co-supporters for our voice recitals. I soon found myself looking for opportunities to pass by her dorm so I could chat with her. Music once again placed us on a college worship team that I eventually led. Over Christmas break, I toured with the worship team, playing at schools and venues in the Midwest and on the west coast. All throughout the tour, I kept in touch with this girl that had captured my affections. After a day of playing at three locations, the band was all looking forward to hitting the pool or hot tub. I was actually more interested to see if I'd gotten a reply to my e-mail. Much of our conversation was of the uncertainty in not knowing if either of us would be returning for a second semester, due to finances. Thankfully, everything got worked out for us both to return and we began officially dating. Things progressed quickly, as I fell head over heels for this girl. My second semester composition project was all based on a song for her. I remember being hated in that class because I was the professor's favorite. I didn't even own the text book! The professor finally gave me one when he found out I was reading off someone else's. But my motivation in the class went beyond just getting an "A." I wanted to impress the girl by writing music for her. Unfortunately, things progressed too quickly physically as well. By the end of our freshman year, I had gotten her pregnant, adding yet one more thing to my list of mistakes.

I was a disgrace to my family, I had dishonored her family, and we both had to drop out of college, because we had tarnished the Christian name as well. All my life I had been quoted statistics about my particular demographic. Less than half of Hispanic males even graduate high school and less than half of those then go on to college. The majority of that number drops out, making the graduation rate only about 12% of Hispanics. I kept hearing my dad's voice in my head, saying I'd ruined my life. At this particular point, I felt like another statistic of a Latino drop-out, destined to work menial jobs in order to pay child support; never amounting to anything. However, that stubborn ambition I mentioned earlier wouldn't let me settle for that. Maybe I missed the boat on my education, but I was not going to be a statistic of a deadbeat dad. I did love this young lady and I was willing to do whatever it took to make it work. I asked Cathi to marry me and she agreed. The resulting conversations with our parents were not fun at all. I remember going to talk to my parents first. My dad sat in silence, then walked off, still not saying anything. For the first time in my life, I wanted him to yell at me. I guess I figured if he yelled at me, then we could move past it. But he said nothing. Cathi's dad, on the other hand, had plenty to say. It started off as mostly talking about his desire to beat me senseless, but he changed his tone from anger to concern for our future. We talked about providing for the family and the difficulty that was ahead. Cathi's conversations with her sisters were met with anger and disappointment as well. We felt the weight of isolation and chastisement. But Cathi's mother came around and led the others to help us put together a nice wedding in just a few months.

We married a year after we met on August 11, 2001. I was 19 and Cathi was 18 years old. Almost 18 years later, we are evidence of God's redemptive power. He took something we messed up and He made it something beautiful. But at the beginning of this story, I thought of myself as damaged goods. How could someone like me be in ministry?

....

Soon after we got married, we moved in with my parents. The relationship with my dad was very strained at this point. I'd already made things tense when I had run away and then gone to the military. But this was just a slap in the face for my parents. My dad was a pastor. My failures were like a stain on his reputation and on the family name. I know he felt humiliated being in front of a congregation, teaching the Word while his first-born son was making a mess of his life.

Dad was the second pastor of a church plant in the south side of Chicago. It was located in a rather rough part of the city where gang wars are commonplace and homelessness rampant. It was a small church that had been meeting in some rented space until my dad came on board. They found an old medical building that they fixed up for the church. It was a small congregation of thirty to forty people, mainly white, though a few Hispanics and one African-American family. It was completely different from the church where my dad had done his pastoral internship, which was in the suburbs, owned their own building, and was primarily Asian. Thinking about going to his church for the first time since our wedding was very awkward. I thought of walking into the cold cinder block building and the coldness of people's staring gazes. We braced ourselves for the humiliation that we knew was coming. We knew people would cast glances in judgment and disgust. We prepared ourselves for the isolation we would feel, the guilt, and the shame. But it never came. Instead of the coldness of shame, we were greeted with the warmth of community. They asked Cathi how far along she was and when she was due. Some asked if we'd thought of names. Others asked if we had everything we needed for the baby. They hugged us and loved on us fiercely. We were overwhelmed by love.

I had worked for one of the elders of that church while I was attending Trinity. Jerome owned a business that bought HUD houses in Chicago, fixed them up, then sold them to low-income families at great deals. I worked on one of his crews doing mostly demolition and drywall, but got the opportunity to learn how to tile, roof, and a slew of other things that came in handy later on in life. Jerome came to me and offered me a job again. In addition, he wanted me and Cathi to come to an afterschool kids' club he'd started at the church. We could help kids with their homework, do some activities with them, and maybe have the opportunity to counsel them and speak into their lives. I was confused. Why would anyone want me to speak into their lives or counsel them? He told me I hadn't run away from this; I was facing the consequences of my actions and I was working to make a better tomorrow. He said that was an example all those kids needed to see. Not all of that sunk in at the moment, but I was humbled and once again overwhelmed at the love that was poured out on us as a couple.

Now, I had grown up in the church all my life. My parents were dedicated followers of Christ and they made sure we had all the exposure in the world to the church, to the gospel, and I witnessed their lives of prayer and devotion. I grew up knowing the answers to all the Bible questions and the Christianese that evidenced a godly upbringing. But I can honestly say that none of that was truly internalized. Sure, I believed in God and I knew who Jesus was and what he had done for me. But it wasn't until my first child, Miguel, was born that I can honestly say that I surrendered my life to Christ. I remember holding him in my arms after he was born and thinking that I couldn't be what he needed me to be. Not on my own anyway. If he was going to follow my example, I knew I needed to be following the best example there is. And in that moment, I truly submitted my life to Jesus.

After some months, I was invited to play guitar for the worship band. Again, I didn't understand why they would ask someone like me to join in leading others in worship. Even though I'd grown up in the church all my life, this was a new experience for me. I knew stories of people that had fallen into moral failure that faced church discipline in the form of rejection so they would eventually leave. That was my expectation. Yet this church showed me a different way - the biblical way. There wasn't chastisement, berating, or casting aside. Their goal was restoration. Isn't that the gospel message in the first place? This church was a beautiful picture of the body of Christ helping people who had fallen down get back up and see their relationship with God and the church restored. And that's what the church wanted to see in me and Cathi. Restoration.

Restoration is based on God's character. God is love. Encompassed in his love are his benevolence, grace, mercy, and persistence. Each of these characteristics is exercised in bringing someone to restoration in the faith. I can tell you that Cathi and I could see the grace and mercy we were shown through people persistently loving us. As they did so, they pointed to God's character. God stopped at nothing in order to provide a way to be restored to him and the church must echo that same restoration and reconciliation. In what is arguably the Bible's most instructive passage on the matter, Jesus tells us to approach others in their error for their restoration. "If he listens to you, you have gained your brother" (Matthew 18:15b). The process continues for a person who is unwilling to repent, but even when Jesus says to let them be as a Gentile, the end goal is for restoration to occur. The reality is that to continue to treat the offender as a believer is to ignore the fact that there is a real need in that person's life. A church who is unwilling to exercise church discipline is not kind or gracious. It ignores the need for healing as well as it ignores the well-being of the entire church body. And in approaching the process with a posture of gentleness and love, as was done to us, the church sets itself up for being the catalyst for restoration. We had many conversations with people about our sin. But it was never in a condemning or belittling way. It was always in a spirit of love and in a desire to see us fully restored to communion with the Father. Paul writes in Galatians 6:1 that "if anyone is caught in any transgression, you who are spiritual should restore him in a spirit of gentleness." And a church who is willing to do this - a church who wants to see others restored to a right relationship with God - is a church who has a heart for missions.

Even from the beginning, God was influencing us to have this heart for missions – a heart to see others come to enjoy the greatness of God. Although at this point we were still miles away from that mindset, it was the beginning of understanding what it is to be missional, because we had experienced it from the other end.

3 EQUIPPING

Had that church not exercised good church discipline, I don't know that I would be where I am today. They played a huge part in my journey to the mission field, though it was still nowhere in sight at the time. Even after the restoration that took place in my family, with God, and in my marriage, I still would not have considered full-time ministry as a viable option for me.

After things in the Chicago housing market got tough, I needed to find another source of income. I entered the Army in the wake of the 911 terrorist attacks and planned on serving 20 plus years, until retirement. At first, I tried to get back into the Marine Corps, but due to my medical discharge, I could not. However, the Army was willing to allow me enlistment with a doctor's record of examination. Besides being a practical way to provide for my new family, I loved being a soldier and I excelled at it. I began my Army service in April 2002 with Basic and Advanced Individual Training at Fort Sill, Oklahoma; home of the Field Artillery. I advanced quickly through the ranks. Though I started at the bottom of the totem pole as an E-1 Private, I was granted waivers for time in service so that I could promote to Sergeant in less than three years' time. My chain of command recommended that I be afforded the opportunity to commission as an officer. So, the Army sent me (back home) to finish my college degree at the University of Illinois in Chicago, after which I was given the rank of second lieutenant. God had graciously restored my dreams of finishing college along with everything else!

Being in Chicago, near my parents, afforded me the opportunity to patch things up with my dad. He wanted to be involved in his grandkids' lives (we had three kids at this point) and we saw them every weekend. To this day, my dad is one of my best friends and supporters. And it was while living in the Chicago suburbs again for those two years, we joined a nearby church where I served as the worship director. That church played a vital part in my journey to the mission field as well.

The church itself was not incredibly special. It was an unimpressive brick building with a well-kept lawn and manicured bushes out front. The sanctuary had a very traditional look with its wooden pews and large pulpit, center stage. Services brought people dressed in their Sunday best along with those that preferred a more casual appearance, making it a very eclectic gathering. Likewise, the worship was varied from the classic hymns to some more modern choruses. The music itself was not exceptional, but adequate. There was a keyboardist, a bassist, an electric guitarist, and a drummer on an electronic set. The stage was unique in that while it was an elevated platform, it had a musician's pit at the back, where the electric guitarist and bassist stood. There were doors on either side of the stage, leading to the baptismal and stairs to the basement. In the lower level were the Sunday school classrooms, fellowship hall, nursery, and bathrooms. While the congregation was an older group of people, there were some younger couples in the mix as well. What drew us in was the small congregation of nearly 100, which didn't even fill the sanctuary half-way. This gave the church more of a community feel of which we wanted to be a part, given our previous experiences. The church's last pastor had literally just resigned before we visited for the first time. But instead of looking for a new pastor right away, they decided to have an interim pastor, to be assigned by the local conference, to get the church ready for whoever the next pastor would be.

Rev. Dr. Robert Moeller had a difficult task of settling church issues and getting the congregation in a healthy state before installing a permanent pastor. I began my role as worship director of the church just before he arrived. During those two years in Chicago, Pastor Moeller (as he preferred to be called), mentored me as one of his staff members. At the time, I found his mentorship peculiar. Though I was simply the worship leader, he would call me up to take me along on visitations of the sick and elderly. I was only in classes three days a week, while still being paid as a sergeant, so there was no need for a job. That meant I had the time to go with him and have impromptu meetings and be at every event the church had. As I was walking out of class one day, my phone rang. Pastor Moeller called to ask me to accompany him on a visitation of an older lady in our church. I told him I would meet him at the church, which was between the university and my house. On the ride to the lady's house, we talked a little about school, a little about the family, and then a whole lot about Scripture. I don't remember the specifics of what we discussed, but I do remember thinking I didn't understand all the words he used. When we arrived, I remember the delight in this little old lady's face as she welcomed us in. It amazed me that something so simple as dropping by could brighten her day. As an older woman, she couldn't always get out to church. Those weeks, the church would send someone to see her and pray with her. During the visit, I mainly observed as he essentially led this woman through a devotional, listened to her talk for a bit, then offered to pray for her. Then he asked me to pray after him! I remember stumbling through my words and trying to remember what the woman asked prayer for. Though I'd prayed out loud before and prayed with others, it was always in a group of peers and never so personal. It wasn't the last time Pastor Moeller asked me to pray, either, and I became less and less apprehensive of it.

We often met multiple times a week to discuss church services. We would try to coordinate song choice with the message to create a cohesion in the service. The practice of doing that with him is something I carried with me years later in leading worship anywhere. When we kicked off a men's Bible study, he asked me to co-lead with him, though I was clearly the youngest man in the group. We also talked an awful lot about marriage, though that was to be expected. He and his wife were the authors of the book, "For Better, For Worse, For Keeps" and to this day have radio and TV shows as well as speaking engagements on marriage throughout the country. He'd tell some story of a difficulty they'd had in their marriage and turn it into a learning point of how they were able to get through it. All the while I served at this church "simply" leading worship, Pastor Moeller was discipling me and grooming me for full-time ministry. He knew I was in the military. He knew I was on a two-year assignment and headed back to Officer's Basic Course. Yet he clearly heard from God that he was to invest in me in that way and did it. By the end of those two years, though he never said a word to convince me to go into ministry, I was drawn to it. Pastor Moeller was instrumental in my development for the ministry. He exercised the biblical model for discipleship and raising up leaders in the church. And even though his efforts may not have benefitted that church directly, he knew he was investing in the Kingdom of God.

Too often times, discipleship is just another ministry among other programs and activities offered by the church. However, Jesus' highest priority while on earth was to make disciples and he has made it the critical action of the church too. The first church in Acts is recorded as devoting themselves to the teaching of the apostles, to fellowship with one another, to breaking bread together, and to prayer (Acts 2:42). It was a learning environment, though it was not a traditional center of education. They learned by living life together. Discipleship is about living, not just learning. Jesus called his disciples to be imitators of their Master. Paul, after Jesus, modeled discipleship as well. In Philippians 4:9, he writes, "Whatever you have received or learned from me, or seen in me - put into practice. And the God of peace be with you." He was intentional about what he was passing on. Discipleship is not something that happens by accident. Pastor Moeller's intentional discipleship of me took after this model of not only teaching me but also showing me and requiring me to imitate. He wasn't just interested in transferring knowledge. The goal was to teach me a new way of thinking altogether, which led to a transformation. It was an infectious experience. Churches need to be intentional about discipleship and not allow it to become merely a byproduct of other ministries. The most effective churches are those that are intentional about true discipleship.

Discipleship led me to a place where I knew God wanted me in ministry. Before I had even graduated from college, I began drafting my first petition for a branch transfer in the Army. I still had the desire to complete 20 years of military service and retire young. The most logical course of action was to transfer to the chaplain corps and do ministry in the military. Over the course of a few years, my first and second requests for a branch transfer were denied. Not by the chaplain corps - they were chomping at the bit to add another to the undermanned branch of spiritual support for our fighting force. However, the Field Artillery, my controlling branch was also looking at numbers, as well as money invested, and refused to release me from my obligation to them. After those two official requests, I even met unofficially, one-on-one with a branch manager. Again, the response was no. After my commitment to the Army was over, I submitted for and was granted resignation from the

Army, so that I could go into full-time ministry.

4 No Plan B

My military career ended on August 1, 2010. I had entered the service as a private and left the position of a captain, less than a decade later. In between, there was a wealth of discipline, knowledge, and growth that had taken place. I entered as a boy and left as a man. I started out naïve and impressionable, and ended up scarred yet teachable. I began with selfish ambition and left with the conviction of God's will in my life. And as God would have it, many of my experiences in the military prepared me for the missions journey ahead.

For the three years preceding my resignation from the Army, I was serving at Dayspring Community Church in Lawton, Oklahoma. This was my home church before going to Chicago for my bachelor's. I had been on staff as the youth director in 2004 - 2005 when the youth pastor had resigned. I left in 2005 for Chicago and returned in 2007. Dayspring became our church home upon our return to Oklahoma once again. Originally, I was only to be at Fort Sill for six months for the Field Artillery Officer Basic Course (FAOBC), followed by an assignment in Fort Carson, Colorado. We were extremely excited to be stationed somewhere else besides Fort Sill. From all that we had heard, Fort Carson was a great assignment. For that reason, I did not fully engage in ministry at Dayspring. I expected to pick up and leave in six months and though I was sure I would return for the Captain's Career Course and possible command opportunities, that wouldn't be for another few years. However, two weeks before graduation from FAOBC, my orders were changed and I was to remain at Fort Sill. I would be lying if I said that I wasn't disappointed. I had dreams of skiing in the Colorado mountains; I longed for actual winters and mild summers. I'd had enough of the 115-degree Oklahoma sun scorching everything in sight from May to August. I was tired of the not-cold-enough-to-snow winters. God had other plans with me. Two days after I received the amended orders, I received a call from the assistant pastor at Dayspring, asking if I would step back into the youth group to help out. So, in January of 2008, I joined the volunteer staff at Dayspring Community Church once again as the youth director. Later that year, we would hire a new lead pastor who would become another influential mentor in my journey to missions.

Not long after Tim Evans took the position of lead pastor at Dayspring, I entered into another mentoring relationship under his leadership. His methods were quite a bit more subtle than that of Pastor Moeller. First of all, he didn't even have a desk in his office. He had an arm chair that he sat in most of the time and then a red couch where people would sit for counseling. Of course there is nothing magical about the red couch, though many lamented its departure when Tim got new furniture. But there are a lot of memories attached to that red couch and Tim's mentorship of me. I remember sitting on that couch and laughing my butt off, crying my eyes out, and even sitting in thick silence as we talked about life, ministry, and leadership. Towards the end of 2009, I remember talking about my desire to continue into full-time ministry and what the next steps were. I had applied and been accepted into Liberty University Baptist Theological Seminary for a Master of Divinity and was enrolling for classes in January of 2010. Since I would be doing this degree online, we talked about having practical application within my ministry context, access to resources, and a whole slew of things to help me in this next step of pursuing full-time ministry. He talked about the church coming alongside of me and licensing me as a pastor when I started seminary.

But then, fast forward to 2010, when I was preparing to leave the military. During this transitional period, I had been looking for another job for that interim period between military and ministry. In this process, I got an offer from an agency that places junior military officers into corporate jobs. The positions that they placed into were on a fast track to management positions. They guaranteed that I would start off making decent money and within 5 years be in a top-tier position, making a six-figure salary. The catch was that you had to be willing to go anywhere they wanted you to go. Often times, you trained for 5 years in one location, then when you promoted to VP, they sent you to another part of the US to oversee another site. They set up the interviews with your best-matched companies and prepped you for the interviews and everything. If for some reason you didn't get hired, the placement company would hire you. Either way, I was guaranteed a great job when I left the military.

I remember sitting on that red couch and telling Tim about the contract they sent me in the mail. It was a deal that was too good to be true – only it was true! All I had to do was sign. And I couldn't. Something within me kept me from putting pen to paper. Tim listened to me talk about the deal and then said something to the effect of, "Look, that's an awesome deal. You'd be a fool not to sign it. Except if you know that God has called you to do something else. Last year you sat in here and you talked about going into full-time ministry. Has that changed?"

The calling hadn't changed, of course, and that's why I couldn't sign the contract. I knew what God was asking of me and signing that contract would be like Jonah taking a boat to Tarshish instead of heading to Nineveh. Tim knew that, too, but instead of telling me outright, he affirmed my calling to ministry. One of the hardest things I'd done in my life up to that point was to take that contract and put it through the shredder. We were cutting the lifeboats and relying on God's plan for our life. There was no plan B.

5 HAITI

After being licensed by the elder board of Dayspring Community Church, I also transitioned from being the youth pastor to an assistant pastor role. In the youth group, I started off leading the group in worship with my guitar. Slowly, musicians began to emerge from the group and I started building a band with the teens. Eventually, I identified some of the teens that had leadership potential and worked with them to take over the band. That was one of the most satisfying things I did in my role as a youth pastor: to empower teens to lead others in worship. Towards the end of my time as a youth pastor, I was asked to lead worship for the church in Sunday morning services. Eventually, this led into the transition to assistant pastor with one of my primary roles as the worship director.

Around the same time that I started seminary, another significant event happened. On January 12, 2010, a massive earthquake measuring 7.0 on the Richter scale hit the country of Haiti, killing thousands and displacing many more. There was so much coverage in the news of the devastation that you had to have been living under a rock to not hear of it. This would prove to be a catalyst for another major change in my life. It began to set our hearts on the country we would later call home.

As Cathi and I heard the news of the earthquake, we began to pray for the victims and the country of Haiti. We began praying as a family for the families affected. Our family consisted of Miguel who was just 8 years old, Kayla at 6, Sandra was 4, and Isaac barely one-year old. We prayed for Haiti at our mealtimes and bedtimes. At some point after we had begun praying, Kayla approached us and said she wanted to do something for the kids of Haiti. She wanted to send them all her stuffed animals to help cheer them up. This was my six-year-old! My initial reaction was that my heart melted. Soon thereafter, the thought struck me that this wasn't a very practical idea. So, how do I redirect this six-year-old without killing her heart and spirit? We settled on doing a garage sale and sending the money to Haiti, rather than parting with the stuffed animals that she couldn't sleep without!

Kayla did all the leg work on her own. She told everyone of the garage sale that she was putting on and even walked around with a glass jar. It had a label that said, "$ For Haiti Kids" on it. Some people just put money in the jar and others offered up items that she could sell in the garage sale. Neighbors and people who weren't even part of our church brought stuff by. And we're not talking just books and CD's. People were giving her bow flexes and nice furniture! They would drive by the house and drop it off, right up to the day of the sale. We helped Kayla organize and price the donations and then that morning, she was up bright and early to help us sell the stuff. She's always been a social butterfly, but that morning she was in her element. Kayla would walk up to people and strike up conversation. When they heard she was the one who organized the garage sale and what it was for, they just caved. I mean, who can resist a six-year-old girl wanting to send money to Haiti to help needy kids? If that's not a pull on your heart strings, I don't know what is. When the day was done and we'd sold most of what was in that garage, Kayla had raised over six hundred dollars. We couldn't believe it! Cathi and I talked about how to send the money down and had settled on an organization we'd worked with for years. We sponsored and become Advocates through Compassion International and though none of our sponsored kids were in Haiti, Compassion was active there. We could send the donations through them to go to their relief efforts after the earthquake. Kayla was beaming.

Fast forward one year later and Cathi was preparing for a youth event at the church called the 30 Hour Famine, organized by World Vision. The event is a thirty hour fast from food as a group. During those thirty hours, the group comes together to study Scripture, pray, and worship together. At the end of the thirty hours, they break the fast together. The event is done as a fundraiser for those that are starving in the majority world. Often times, the Bible studies as part of "The Famine" center on what it means to be spiritually hungry, while also looking at the hunger epidemic in the world. I offered to be part of the event to lead worship and lead some of the Bible studies. So, I began to look at the material that World Vision sent. As a result of the earthquake the previous year, World Vision was choosing to focus all their material on Haiti in 2011. My heart broke for the people again as I read statistics of the country. As I prepared for the event, I prayed even more for Haiti and for its people. During the 30 Hour Famine, we prayed and fasted together for Haiti. For some time after the event, we continued to pray and fast for Haiti.

Interestingly enough, that year God also began to shape my heart for ministry. As I studied the Scriptures, theology, and ministry in seminary, I began to realize that I didn't have a desire to become the lead pastor of a church in America. First, I was scared to death to get up every Sunday morning in front of hundreds of people and sing and play the guitar. The only reason I did it was because I lose myself in worshiping God and I just invited others to worship with me. But I was not a great public speaker, nor comfortable in front of a crowd. I am an introvert that would be quite content sitting by myself, studying. My gifts, talents, and passions did not line up with a lead pastor position. These thoughts landed me on the red couch yet again to discuss this with Tim. As we talked more and more, we explored my upbringing. I was born in Puerto Rico in a culture different from the one that I was in. I grew up speaking Spanish and kissing people to greet them. As I moved to the States, I became a kid in between cultures (a third-culture kid, as others have called it). I had my foot in two different cultures. My parents sent me back to the island every chance they had - for summer break, Christmas, and sometimes more. To this day, I still speak to my mother in Spanish even though she speaks English just fine. There were some elements of my culture that just stayed, even as I adopted American ones. Fast forward through the military, where I travelled to other cultures, but more than that, worked and lived in community with others. The thought of going to another culture to share the Word of God was an exciting idea. The idea of missions took hold in my head and heart and I began to look at future ministry in that light. I even changed the concentration of my degree from pastoral ministry to missional studies. I got excited about studying cultural anthropology and cross-cultural ministry.

By the end of 2011, Cathi made a transition from youth ministry to the missions board of our church. Dayspring had affirmed our desire to enter into missions and as a result, Cathi was getting her hand in it from this angle. She is a very good administrator and as a result, was asked by the board to put together an international short-term missions trip for the church to engage in 2012. As God would have it, the trip was to Haiti.

With both of us now looking at a future in missions, Cathi and I saw this trip as an opportunity to expose the family to missions and get our feet wet. We decided to take our two oldest, Miguel and Kayla, along with us to Haiti. In my mind, I was set on doing something in South America - or at least some Spanish-speaking country. That was my first language, so it seemed like a no-brainer to me. In fact, Cathi and I already had our "dream assignment" for missions. She had returned to school to study nutrition science and had just graduated. Her concentration was malnutrition in developing countries. Put together with over eight years of experience in child sponsorship Stateside, we wanted to partner with Compassion International overseas. Since Compassion always works through the local church, I was excited about empowering local church leaders and providing support to them. We had no idea if that was even a possibility, but it was our dream, nonetheless. I was holding out for a Hispanic country and Cathi was not so secretly wanting to go to Africa. And of course, we weren't ready to go yet. I hadn't finished seminary yet, so we had to wait at least until that was done. So, no; Haiti was not on our minds as an option for missions.

We arrived at Nehemiah Vision Ministries (NVM) in Chambrun, Haiti on August 1, 2012. We were greeted at the airport by one of the interns and shuttled to the campus about 45 minutes away in a large transport truck. There were still tell-tale signs of the earthquake in places as we drove - crumbled buildings, mostly. But there was less and less of that as we kept driving past little towns and populated areas until we were finally in the open, driving towards a mountain range. With what seemed to be civilization behind us, we turned on a dirt road that had a sign for the ministry. A mile later of bouncing up and down on the rocky terrain and inhaling the dust that flew up from the dry ground, we turned into the guarded campus of Nehemiah Vision Ministries. We were in the middle of nowhere. Or so it seemed to us. There was cactus all around, sparse vegetation, and the sun scorching everything. The only electricity and water there was provided by the generator on campus. The community had neither of their own. Yet, despite these unwelcoming conditions, we were excited to be there and serve in whatever capacity we could.

As we got off the transport in the team center, I noticed the buildings on that side of the campus resembled some of our temporary military tents used on deployments and field operations. They were more than tents, set on concrete pads, with metal beams holding the sturdy canvas in an arc overhead. Our team of 30 was ushered inside the dormitories, which really reminded me of military barracks. There were about fifty bunks inside the men's dorm and we quickly placed our suitcases on some nearby beds. Just across the front door to the dorm, we would walk to the cafeteria, where our sheets, pillow cases, and towels awaited us on a table. After taking them back to the dorm, we reconvened in the cafeteria to receive our orientation. There was some cultural awareness in the briefing, as well as some general house rules.

After all of that, the staff member proceeded to tell us some of the needs of the ministry. Among other things, they were praying for a staff member in Haiti to coordinate the child sponsorship program, a nurse for their malnutrition program, and a pastor to help in their pastoral development program. Cathi and I looked at each other with inquisitive looks. God was affirming our passions and desires for missions. Just not in our desired context...

Later that year, in November, Cathi and I found ourselves in Haiti for the second time. We were supposed to have gone to Peru to check out some ministry positions there, but when the plans fell through, we ended up in Haiti instead. While there, we wrestled with the idea of doing full-time missions with them. There were some days we engaged in some service with the Haitian staff. We did odd jobs here and there during the course of the week, but the bulk of our time was spent in prayer. We walked the campus and prayed for the ministry; we met with leaders and staff and we later prayed for them; we saw the needs of the community and we spent time in prayer for them. But we saw where we could fit into the ministry and we prayed for God's leading. By the end of the week, we had an invitation from Pastor Pierre, the president and founder, to join the staff. Before making an affirmative decision, we decided to go home and talk with our kids first.

Back at home, the family sat around the dining room table. I put a basket in the center of the table, then gave everyone a little piece of paper and a pen. As I looked at our kids (then ages 10, 8, 6, and 3), I told them that I wanted to hear what they had to say. We were going to write on the paper "yes" if we thought that this was where God was leading our family and "no" if that wasn't the case. We weren't voting on whether we thought it would be cool to live in another country or if it would be fun or even if it sounded like a good idea. We wanted to vote on whether we thought that God was calling us to go to Haiti. If so, then we only had the choice to obey or disobey. So, we prayed first, then put our votes in the basket. When I pulled the papers out, it was unanimously decided that this was where God wanted our family - which meant we were moving to Haiti!

6 EASY

Soon after arriving in Haiti, I met a man who goes by the name of Easy. He had been hired by Nehemiah Vision Ministries (NVM) to be the head of security, since he had experience as a former police officer. As I got to know him, he showed interest in being mentored by me. It was a mutually edifying relationship. He helped me get to know Haitian culture and the language better while I was helping him develop spiritually. After nearly a year, he left the security job to drive a moto. Here in Haiti, most of transportation is done by either tap-tap or moto. A tap-tap is a pick-up truck or larger vehicle that has been outfitted to be a people mover. Typically benches are added to the back and a covering placed over the bed of the truck. A moto is simply a motorcycle. Those are cheaper to purchase than a four-wheeled vehicle and they can get around traffic jams pretty well. Essentially, they're both used in the same fashion as a taxi service. A moto ride is more expensive, but it's faster than a tap-tap. Plus, it's not a set route. They're wheels for hire. Easy had saved up enough money to get a moto and he could earn pretty decent money doing this. He still came to church services on our campus and much of his clientele was coming or going to our campus. This afforded us the opportunity to keep meeting. However, some months into this new line of work, I got a call in the middle of the night. It was his wife, Leah. With a shaky voice, she told me that Easy had been arrested and taken to jail.

A few days later, I drove up to the jail where they were holding Easy. The cell was a concrete room, maybe twelve feet by twelve feet with iron bars. That was literally it. There were no beds, no toilet, nothing. His cell mate was laying on a woven mat that had been brought in for him. Easy didn't have so much as a sheet to wrap up in or a pillow to put his head on. In the corner of some cells I saw a bucket. The stench in that hallway gave away what they were for. Apparently, some inmates were allowed to use the bathroom at the end of the hall under guard, while others were not. The jail fed the inmates once a day minimal rations. Anything else, their family and friends needed to bring in for them. If they didn't have anybody to help them, the once a day jail food is all they got. Easy was glad to see me, but as soon as I asked what had happened to land him there, his countenance changed. He told me the events of what happened, but the story he relayed to me was more like a defense before a jury. Pride and anger had replaced the joy and peace in him. One of his regular fares had been short some money when he took him home one day. Easy told him he could pay him the next time he gave him a ride. The man avoided Easy until one night when he needed a ride home. As he got off the moto, he went to pay for the ride. When Easy saw that he'd been shorted again, he punched the man and knocked some teeth out of his mouth. Others nearby called the police and they arrested Easy. His anger was still fresh when I saw him in his cell that day. He felt he was justified for hitting the man. He felt insulted that he would not pay him the full fare twice in a row. I let him know that I did not visit him to side with him, but to show him that I love him, let him know I was still there for him, and we would take care of his family. He thanked me and I prayed with him before I left.

The next visit, I brought him a Bible as he'd requested. I brought one along as well so that we could look at some Scripture together. After looking and talking about a passage, Easy told me that they were telling him he had to pay for the man's dental bill or pay to go to trial. If he couldn't do either, he would sit in jail until he could. That, of course, was not likely, since he wasn't making any money sitting in that cell. Either way, he needed about a thousand dollars that he didn't have. It looked like he would be in there for some time. I told him that I couldn't pay that, but that I would pay for his next six month's rent to make sure his family didn't have to worry about it. Leah had two kids, a boy and a girl not quite school-age, to take care of. We prayed again before I left and I asked that God would help him to learn what he needed to in this season of life. That would be my last visit. Once it was clear that he wouldn't be able to pay, they moved Easy to another facility with extremely limited visitation.

The congregation rallied around Leah, who was highly involved in the church. People would volunteer to watch the kids for her so that she could take food to Easy each day. The church gave her boxes of fortified rice to ensure that they were getting something to eat. All the while, her faith stayed strong. She prayed for her husband, knowing he needed a change to happen in his life. Eight months later, Easy was released from prison, a new man.

In the few months that passed since his release, I witnessed a new hunger in him for the Word of God, a renewed commitment to provide for his family, and a return of that lost joy in life. During the time he was in jail, his license and registration for the motorcycle had expired. We started working on a way to get him those back so that he can fully provide for his family again. One of the foundational philosophies of ministry in Haiti is to empower people, not make them dependent on anyone else. In that light, Easy and I talked about how we could get him back up on his feet. After praying through the situation, I didn't feel paying for all of it outright was what he needed, but I didn't want him to think I had abandoned him in this, either. One night, he called me and he said, "I have an idea." He asked me if I would loan him the equivalent of $20, so that he could start up a side business of selling pre-paid minutes for the Haitian cellular network, Digicel. Then, after paying me back, he would continue to get the money he needed for his license and registration. I told him to come over. As I gave him the 1,000 gourdes note, I told him he didn't have to pay this back. I was happy to make that small investment.

Little did I know that Easy would come to be a part of some major transitions for my family in Haiti. Later, he became the nighttime security guard at our home in the community.

7 DANGEROUS PRAYERS

Only a couple of months after arriving in Haiti, I'd taken up a prayer of asking God for opportunities to show His love to people in meaningful ways. Sometimes, this has been as simple as giving a mom with her little ones a ride to the clinic. However, on one particular day, this prayer turned into a much bigger adventure.

I was driving back from the airport in our JAC (little tap-tap). Miguel was sitting next to me in the cab and Cathi was in the back with the rest of our children and the four people we had just picked up from the airport. We stopped at the first stop light on our route and, as usual, kids at the intersection began asking us for money. One came up to my window and I was looking at him. When I looked over at Miguel's window, the boy on that side had jumped in through the window into the JAC up to his waist and grabbed my iPhone sitting on the seat next to Miguel, then took off running behind us. I did what I felt any good Haitian would do... I put the parking brake on and ran after him. There was a street vendor behind our vehicle and I asked him, "Kote li te ale?" (Where did he go?) He pointed down the street and I took off in that direction. I ran by a man who started talking to me, asking, "¿Hablas español? ¿Que pasó?" (Do you speak Spanish? What happened?). I said, "Un muchacho me robó el telefono" (A boy stole my phone). He then took off in that direction, too as I was stopped by policeman on a motorcycle who asked me, "Sak pase?" (What's going on?) to which I responded, "Yon gason te vole telefon mwen" (A boy stole my phone). He turned his moto around and took off down the street. I kept running up the street and the man and the police had caught up to the boy and had him off the road (we were literally running down the street). I thanked the Hispanic, who asked me, "¿De donde eres?" After I told him I was from Puerto Rico, he went back in the direction we'd come. (We are next to the Dominican Republic, so it's not all that strange to run into Spanish speakers.) The police asked me again what had happened and I told him, "Li te vole telefon mwen. Li ble ak nwa." (He stole my phone. It's blue and black). The policeman reached into the boy's pocket and found my phone there. He proceeded to essentially spank this kid, who was about 13 years old.

By this time, we had quite a gathering of UN officers around us, inquiring as to what had happened. I was questioned by a UN officer from India, another from the Cote d'Ivoire, and various Haitian police. The police asked me to stick around so they could get my report. At this point, I asked if I could go and at least park my vehicle somewhere, since it was still at the intersection. So I ran back to the intersection, hopped in the JAC and drove it across the intersection to a gas station. I then ran back to where they had the kid in custody. He was now with his hands on a wall and legs spread apart, with a police officer holding him by the back of his pants. I waited there for another half hour before a police car showed up, in which they put the boy and then asked me to follow to the police station. I drove the JAC a ways to the station, where I parked it once again and went in. At this time, they had me give an official statement. As I was doing so, I noticed the jail cell adjacent to that room, where there were quite a few people, inquisitively looking on. They did not seem like very friendly people. The police then explained to me that they would like to press charges on this kid to have him spend a few nights in jail, but in order to do that, they needed my cooperation. I looked back at the cell and back at this 13-year-old kid and did not think that was a great idea. Instead, I asked the police officer if I could talk to him. He almost chuckled, but said fine. I then walked up to the kid and told him that the police wanted me to give them what they needed to keep him in jail. His eyes grew big at the realization. I then proceeded to tell him that I didn't want that to happen; I told him I forgave him and wanted him to be a better person because God had made him to do something better with his life. I told him he could be helping people instead of taking advantage of them. I told him that when the police let him go, it was his choice to do something good with himself, but only God would know if he did. I told him I believed in him. After I talked, the boy looked me in the eye and apologized.

I told the police officer I didn't want him to spend the night in jail and that he could let him go. He asked me if I was sure I wanted to do that. He tried to talk me into letting them press the charges, because otherwise, the kid was just going to do it again. I told the officer that there was a better chance of him doing it again after being in jail; nobody's probably ever given this kid a reason to do anything good with his life and I hoped that he'll remember this next time he thinks about stealing. The police officer actually did chuckle at me this time. First, he asked me how long I'd been in Haiti. When I told him three months, he asked how I'd learned Creole! I told him I learned by talking to Haitians, how else?! He then grabbed my phone, put his number in it and as he gave it back to me, he said, "My name is Reginald. You're a good person. If you're ever in trouble, you can call me and I'll help." I walked out of the station unsure of how to feel. It dawned on me that this was one of the most tangible ways that kid would understand God's redeeming love. And I prayed that this crazy afternoon would make a long-lasting impact on him.

Two weeks later, I saw him at the same street corner. Only this time he had a bottle of water in one hand and a squeegee in the other, going from car to car, asking if he could wash their windshield for change. When he got to my car, he laughed as he recognized me. We exchanged greetings and he proceeded to clean my windshield. As I gave him some change and drove off, I silently thanked God and prayed again for this kid's future. I saw him a few more times at that intersection until that traffic light was no longer functioning. My prayers to this day for him are that he reaches the potential for which God created him.

It is a wonder to me that the God of the universe who

created everything and is sovereign over all would establish prayer as a means for His will to be accomplished. Nevertheless, it is a reality that God wants our prayers and accomplishes His will as we pray for it to be fulfilled. Jesus, as he taught his disciples to pray, says, "May your will be done on earth as it is in heaven." His own life was marked by prayer as he sought to do the Father's will and not his own. Before choosing the 12 disciples, Scripture tells us that Jesus spent the whole night in prayer. Then, he chose those the Father had given him. The night of his betrayal, Jesus agonized in prayer and asked that he be spared from the suffering that would follow. Yet he surrendered his desires to the will of the One who sent him. You see, prayer is more about accomplishing God's will than asking Him to do ours. And certainly during our time in Haiti, I learned more and more about the power of prayer – not just my own prayers, but those of others for us as well.

8 SPIRITUAL WARFARE

At the root of spiritual warfare is the battle for God's glory. We have an enemy that seeks to steal, kill, and destroy. Since we are the pinnacle of God's creation and bearers of his image, it's no wonder that we find ourselves in the midst of these conflicts. However, the manifestation of this spiritual warfare can certainly look different from culture to culture. Most people would agree that Haiti is full of spiritual warfare, due to the worship of spirits, sacrifices to other gods, and the voodoo culture in general. This isn't to say that there is no spiritual warfare at play in the United States. One of the things that hit me like a ton of bricks on several return trips to the US is the oversexualization in this culture. Everything is sensualized. Particularly for men, this is a daily battle in spiritual warfare for our purity. That's just one example of the manifestation in this context. In Haiti, the voodoo culture and mentality that it has created presented its own challenges to doing ministry. The following are blog posts during my time in Haiti pertaining to this unique struggle.

Voodoo Tree

The village of Chambrun is a mud-hut village with no running water and no electricity, situated just half a mile from the gates of NVM. The village is also steeped in voodoo. There are multiple voodoo temples with many followers. Voodoo beliefs center on the idea that there is a supreme being, Bondye, that created the world, but then stepped back and is not accessible by the human race. He also created lesser gods or spirits (*lwa*) endowed with divine power and authority. They believe it is through these *lwa* that people connect with Bondye. In that light, voodooists will worship many *lwa*, some of which are territorial, some ancestral, and others of a more universal nature. Appeasing these spirits is how they believe they get favor with the creator god. Conversely, upsetting these spirits also earns them judgment and retribution.

In many villages, where there are centers of voodoo, there is typically a tree that is associated with their worship. These trees are believed to be embodied by at least one *lwa* if not multiple spirits. They are sacred trees to the people and they take care of them. There are multiple stories floating around of people who tried to chop down these trees and had axes and machetes bounce off and cut their legs instead. This goes to show their belief that these trees are protected by the spirits themselves. Their voodoo ceremonies typically take place under these trees, giving even more cultural or religious significance to these trees. A lot of times, there will be glass bottles hanging from its branches. Sometimes, you may even find a chair hanging! These items are used in "cleansing rituals" where an individual who is sick, for example, is cleansed of their malady. If they're sitting on a chair during the ritual, the chair is then hung on the tree to air out and allow the sickness to come off it. The bottles have the same idea in trapping the sickness or bad spirit within it once it leaves a person.

One such tree sits in the middle of the village of Chambrun. There are several others, but this particular tree is big. There is no bigger tree in Chambrun. In fact, the sight of such a large tree is strange, since Chambrun is known for making charcoal. Typically, trees don't get large enough to produce branches larger around than my wrist because they are chopped down to make charcoal. However, in the case of a voodoo spirit tree, they wouldn't dare cut it down. Unless you're me.

To be fair, it was an accident. My kids were all part of a group that is a cross between Boys/Girls' Scouts and Awanas. It's an extension of the Christian Brigade that began in Chicago. On the group's anniversary every year, they parade through the village and in the surrounding area as a celebration. They have very choreographed marches that look more like dances as they walk. It was very neat to watch. So, during the march of 2014, I was driving the personnel truck, following the group. I was carrying water in the back for those that needed to rehydrate. Those that needed a break from the marching could also hop in and rest, then hop back out and join the group when they were ready. The group turned off the road down the trail to the center of Chambrun. They were going to march straight through the village and out the next one. As

I followed behind, I saw the large voodoo tree up ahead to the right. I paid no mind and just kept rolling along. As I passed the under some of the branches of the tree, I misjudged the height of the truck. I had forgotten there was a luggage rack on top that made it stick up quite a bit farther. As a result, I heard a big CRACK as the rather thick branch from the tree broke off and fell to the ground with a big thud. Immediately, people came out of the voodoo temple next door and began shouting obscenities at me. I apologized profusely and offered to help them clean it up. They would have none of it. I might have even asked if someone could use it to make charcoal, which I'm sure was even more insulting. They continued the yelling and cursing at me to the point that I couldn't even make out one person's words over another's. One of the church leaders came to my rescue and explained it was not intentional, but an accident and I'm pretty sure he even pulled the "blan" card in saying that I didn't know any better because I was a foreigner. Finally, the one I assume was the temple's voodoo priest called an actual curse on me and turned back to go inside. We both shrugged our shoulders. I now realized that several people from the community were standing outside their homes, watching the commotion. I grabbed the pieces of the branch that were still on top of the truck and tossed them on the ground as they all looked on. Then, I resumed the march.

Over the next few months, as I continued to visit the village and friends there, I noticed there seemed to be chattering and whispering going on whenever I walked by. On one such occasion, I was there with one of my Haitian friends, so I asked him what was going on. He cracked a smile and said,

"They are talking about you still being alive. They say the spirits aren't able to kill you, because you're connected to a higher power." I thanked God for the tangible expression of his power to them, though it was a completely foreign concept to me.

Halloween In Haiti

Many of my experiences in the military prepared me for overseas missions. Additionally, ministry opportunities in multiple church settings also helped to equip me for international ministry. Some of this equipping was intentional by other parties - such as mentors and the church. Other parts of my equipping were not intentional, yet still orchestrated by God, who ultimately knows what I would need. After being in Haiti for about a year and a half, there came a situation that evidenced the equipping that had taken place in my life.

While American Halloween is iconized by trick or treating, Haiti lives out the reality of what that represents. On November 1 and 2, voodoo practitioners go to cemeteries and gravesites to pray to spirits, offer food, light candles, and dance through the night. During these days, celebrations are conducted in the voodoo tradition, in which people honor Baron Samedi, the god of the dead, and his offspring, Gede. These celebrations are called Fête Gédé. During these ceremonies, people seek to be possessed by these voodoo gods as they honor the dead. It is not uncommon for people to leave a church service and head to the graveyard to participate in these festivities. Unfortunately, there is a lot of syncretism (mixing of religions) involved with voodoo, particularly with Catholicism. The Catholic tradition of praying for the souls of those in purgatory finds a home amidst the voodoo festivities honoring the dead. Many Haitians would say that while Catholicism and Protestantism were brought in, it is voodoo that is their own and connects them in a common identity. This tends to be a rather tumultuous time in Haiti.

I was invited to an evangelistic crusade that began the Sunday before the weekend of Halloween and All Saints' Day. I was asked to participate on the opening night by offering a prayer towards the beginning of the program. The event itself was hosted on private property – not in a church, but in someone's walled-in yard of pretty good size. The gate to the property was open, so that people could wander in as they passed by. In the yard, they had built a stage, standing about four feet high. Next to the stage were huge speakers that got cranked up so that all in the neighborhood and probably in the next one over could hear what was going on. Some benches were brought in from nearby churches for people to sit on. Others brought in personal chairs. Many others just stood during the entire service. I got there prior to the start, so that I could pray with the leadership and staff of the event for God to use the efforts to draw people to Himself and that He would have His way with the service that evening. Little did I know what that would mean for me.

The band played a worship song to start off and had me pray afterwards. As I walked off the stage, I planned on leaving in the middle of the service, to try and get home before it got too dark. About fifteen minutes before that, I got a call from a friend, saying that he was trying to get to the crusade, but couldn't find a ride. So, I left to pick him up and brought him to the service. When I returned, they were still going strong, singing worship songs. It was already about when I had planned to leave. At this point, the one who organized the event came up to me and said the speaker they had scheduled for that evening had not shown up. So, he asked me if the speaker didn't show up in ten minutes, if I could give the message. Talk about being put on the spot!

Fifteen minutes later, they handed me the microphone and I began giving the simple gospel message for those that were gathered there that evening. I was completely surprised that for such a large crowd, it was quiet as they sat or stood, listening to the gospel. I had no notes and no preparation, yet the words flowed as if I'd prepared all week. I was grateful for an evangelism experience a few weeks ago, going door to door in Village Casimir. I thanked God for the experience of more than a year of preaching on Sundays and leading pastors' conferences, teaching the Word. God had already equipped me for that night. Between seminary, ministry experience at previous churches, and recent events in Haiti, I had been equipped. At the end of the message, I prayed for the people and there were those that prayed to receive Christ that evening. It wasn't my doing – I just happened to be in the place God wanted me to be that night; He changed my plans and used me to do His will.

Easter

During Holy Week in Haiti, there are many Haitian voodoo ceremonies and practices; perhaps the most significant of these being the *rara*. Very plainly, a *rara* is a procession with loud music that is steeped in idolatry and spiritual symbolism. On the surface, they seem like such a fun and harmless piece of Haitian culture, with the colorful dress and upbeat music. Underneath, the full picture cannot be divorced from the worship of voodoo gods. Each *rara* group/band that goes out is under the protection and thus, dedicated, to a *lwa* or god. Some *raras* are formed through family lineage and are done to honor ancestors who are believed to walk with the *rara* procession. Motivations to start *raras* range from political to religious reasons. Many start *raras* to increase their popularity or reputation in a given area. It is a loud walking advertisement. Other *raras* start just for fun, as young people see the older generations. However, all *raras* are eventually "claimed" by a *lwa* and become angaje "under contract" to the deity. There are cases of children starting a *rara* for fun only to be claimed by the family lwa and told that they must go out on public processions to please them. In most of these cases where the *rara* is claimed, the lwa inform the members of the *rara* through a possessed person that they want to adopt the group. Through these *raras*, the people are serving that god. The *raras* are then usually either led by a voodoo priest or at least endorsed by one. Once the group is "under contract", they must go out for seven years or risk upsetting the god, who will inflict disease, misfortune, and even death on its members and even their families. On the other side, if they are faithful and conduct the *raras* in their honor, the *lwa* protects them, blesses them financially, or ensures a successful harvest, etc. These *raras* intensify throughout the week and culminate with an all-night procession Friday to Saturday, as if to celebrate some victory.

It's no surprise then that the local church has a culturally relevant rebuttal to this. Sunday morning, as we celebrate Jesus' resurrection, the church goes on long marches around villages and whole areas to proclaim that Jesus is alive! It's as if to say in reply, "Wait! You're missing the best part of the story…" Around 4am—before sunrise, they begin gathering and walking. They're usually accompanied by a sound system that plays music and people are singing and dancing through the streets, urging others to join in the celebration of the resurrection. Others join and make the roughly five mile walk/dance which culminates in an outdoor service. It's a neat and effective way that the church takes a stand against the culture and invokes a counter-culture to proclaim the truth.

This made me think about American culture as it pertains to the culture of the church. Culture wants to be free to respond to their surroundings and life as they encounter it, rather than be subject to the confines of a belief-system. American society would rather respond than believe. This is a short-circuit approach to religion. This has also led to a secularized Christianity. Today's culture has made Christianity a situation of response and interpretation, rather than a case of belief. People cannot reconcile a belief that claims objective truth, rendering all others false, null, and invalid. In the process, our culture has made sin look normal and righteousness look weird. While culture may have been what reminded us of our sin and separation from God, it has lost the ability of functioning this way.

Our society banks on the idea that everyone has the right to make their own choices. Contemporary society wants to be free to make their own choices and to not feel guilty about them. Therefore, Christianity is regarded as an institution outside these limitations that culture has established. People who cling to this ideal come to a significant opposition with a figure that says, "I am the way and the truth and the life. No one comes to the Father except through me" (John 14:6). And although this is not a discussion on free-will, the point is that people want to make certain that their choices are not infringed upon. They want their freedom. But the world's definition of freedom is erroneously based on a selfish mind-set. And that is the struggle of Christianity within the culture – to paint the picture of what freedom really is. The truth is that real freedom is only possible in Jesus.

The simple answer is that only the Christian mind (enlightened by the Holy Spirit) can make sense of the human condition. Society is showing the signs that it is merely looking for some meaning to life and existence. The real problem has occurred when the church, rather than standing its ground, has followed suit. Culture throws out all these fancy philosophies and ideologies in an attempt to add meaning and try to grasp knowledge. I mean, the message of Jesus Christ is a really simple one. However, we complicate it by making it look like everything else in society. The church has believed that the culture would not penetrate its structure.

However, we see that the values that are prevalent in today's society have permeated the values of the church. Christians see the corruption in the world and refuse to believe it will have any effect on them.

Christ called us to be set apart. And his message transcends all cultures, all languages, and all barriers that mere men could establish. What culture needs to see is the church living out this message in the midst of their chaotic world. There is no middle ground. The church cannot sit idly by and watch the rest of the world develop their culture while pretending to remain unchanged by it. In that event, the church will be swallowed up in it and transformed into something it is not meant to be. This has already started to happen. The church will have no future unless it can speak the language of truth in word and deed. Christians are called to live a life of faithful yet risky discipleship in this world. Without doing this, the church will fail to respond in a redemptive way to the culture around us.

9 GROWING FAITH

When we had moved to Haiti, there were still several things up in the air. We had sold most of what we had, but we had not managed to sell the house. The realtor had suggested that we keep it up for sale, but as we approached the date of our departure, we could also put it up for rent. When we got on the plane for Haiti, it was still available. It wasn't until two days after we were on the ground in Haiti that we received word that someone would be moving in as renters. We could have chosen to wait until the house was taken care of before going. That certainly would have been less stressful. But in this way, God had the opportunity to increase our faith as we followed the plan he'd laid out for us.

The other issue that was unresolved was that of financial support. As missionaries, we had to raise all of our support. Nehemiah Vision Ministries required us to be at least 75% funded before we could book tickets to get down there. We had met that requirement, but we also had to come up with a plan to come up with the rest. Since we were moving in May, we decided we would return to the US in December. That way, we could be with family for the holidays and also do the fundraising we needed to make up the deficit in our support.

Our travels back to Haiti from that fundraising trip were quite rough. It started with a drive from Oklahoma to Michigan since we were flying out of Detroit. This was at the same time there was a big snow storm in the Midwest. I ended up driving through the night to make up for how slow we were going. After a night of sleep, we left for the airport and ended up needing a truck to pull us out of the snow before we'd even left town! The trip to the airport was slow going and, when we were just miles away, we turned onto an off-ramp that was pure ice. Ahead, two cars had already been stranded. One started backing up into on-coming traffic and when I hit the brakes, even at six miles an hour, there was nothing that would stop the van. The back end of our vehicle was heavy with our luggage, so the van turned around and we hit back-end to back-end. Thankfully there was no one seriously injured, though we were nursing backaches for a while. By the time the police came and did their report, we had one hour until take-off. The only way we made our flight was because the gentleman at the curb-side check-in took care of our bags and printed our boarding passes with "TSA pre-check" so that we could get right through security and to our gate. We made it with only 5 minutes to spare! Stress levels were high, but we were thankful to make the flight. We spent the night in Miami and flew out again the following day to arrive in Haiti. After arrival, we got in yet another car accident on the way home from the airport. Nothing serious, but it added to our stress. We arrived on campus to two teams already there, so we hit the ground running.

The day after arriving in Haiti, I went to the airport to pick up yet another team. It was a larger team, requiring the use of our tap-tap, a big box truck turned into a people mover. We had some pretty experienced drivers and the one I had that day is one that I trusted completely. On the way back from the airport, we hit traffic. We have a policy that we won't let vehicles sit with teams in traffic for too long. Following that policy, our driver turned the truck around and took a turn down another road. We followed the bumpy road before trying to take a turn to get back on the main street again. However, three dump trucks were backing out of this alley, so our driver kept on going. Pretty soon, we were in an area that I'd never been before. The road was narrow due to property walls—to the point that no other vehicle could have passed going the other way. The narrow road finally gave way to a downward slope with piles and piles of trash on either side. Eventually, we were driving through the trash. Now, if we'd stayed on the main road, we would have driven over a bridge. But on this bumpy dirt back road, there was no bridge. This was the trash piling up on the side of the river… and we were headed for it down the river bank. We were in the dry season, so the river was at about knee-depth. The driver gunned the engine to get across the river—only he was not trying to get across the river. He was driving along on the river bed to get further down. So, yes, we got stuck. The wheels turned but the vehicle wasn't getting good traction on the river bottom. At one point, the team that was riding in the vehicle all moved to the very back in order to put some weight over the back tires. Finally, the tap-tap got the traction it needed to move and get up the other side of the river bank. Several turns later, I recognized where we were and soon after, we arrived on campus.

Any one of those events is just a bad day... but the string of circumstances kept piling up. I could keep going on events that have happened since we had arrived - literally every day - that threatened to discourage us and beat us down. It should have been no surprise... we were in enemy territory and he didn't like it.

The Visitor

The Friday after getting back to NVM, I received a phone call from a friend in Onaville. At one time, Onaville was the largest IDP camp and tent city in Haiti. After the earthquake, some 600,000 people were displaced to this mountainside. This man lived in Port Au Prince prior to that and was one of those who displaced by the earthquake. NVM had a second campus in Onaville - a 20-minute drive from the one in Chambrun. While I was there visiting one afternoon, I met Mark-Arthur. After telling him I was a pastor with NVM, he got excited and led me to his home, which was on the other side of the mountain. While a large part of Onaville is now made up of cinder block homes, he and his wife were still living in a tent made out of sticks and blankets. When he was displaced there, he quickly realized he was the only Christian in his new surroundings. Rather than be discouraged, he began preaching the gospel. As a result, he saw every one of his neighbors in the immediate area come to Christ. He then began leading all of them in prayer and Bible study each day.

On this Friday, Mark-Arthur called me around lunch time and told me he wanted to come by later that day. Late in the afternoon, I began getting sporadic phone calls from him, asking about the exact location of our campus. He finally called me at 6pm to say that he had arrived. When I went to meet him at the gate, I realized that he had walked the better part of the afternoon to come see me!

I invited him to come have dinner with us in the dining hall. While we ate together, he began telling me of his church and how they were still meeting together at 5pm every night and 6am every Sunday (before the sun gets hot, because they have no building). Then, he asked me to be their pastor. I was floored by this request. At the same time, I was afraid that I would upset him when I turned him down. For the next few moments, I affirmed what he was doing with this group of believers and tried to help him see that he was their pastor! He was very apprehensive to be given that title, because he said he really wasn't a pastor. So, I asked him to be a part of our Pastoral Development Program, where we can give him some tools and resources to help him do what he's already doing in that community. He agreed to come that Saturday to the seminar and insisted that I come to the church on Sunday to visit.

Spendie

As I was preparing to teach one weekend, a friend of mine stopped by the house. Herbie appeared to have been crying and was clearly shaken up. I followed him out to the porch to talk. A few days before, he had stopped by with his little girl,

Spendie, to show us some sores that had developed on her body, particularly on her backside. At that point, he'd been to a clinic, which had given him an ointment and sent him to a hospital that could do further testing. He told me that after that day, he'd taken Spendie to two hospitals and they both told him the same thing: "This isn't a sickness medicine can fix. If you're a Christian, pray; if you're not, take her to a witch doctor." He continued to tell me about heightened voodoo activity in our area (he was one of our neighbors) but that he didn't know who would put a curse on his little girl. In tears, he told me he didn't want to take her to the voodoo temple, because he didn't believe in that stuff. He was a Christian and went to the same church we did. At the same time, he was at whit's end and desperate to help his little girl.

I told Herbie I wanted to go pray for her, so we left my house and walked down the street to his house. There she was, lying on a mat on the floor, visibly uncomfortable. After greeting his wife and others in the house, I talked with them, sympathizing with their situation of watching their child suffer without being able to truly help. I assured them that God sympathized with them too, as he watched Jesus suffer for us. We prayed together, for Spendie, for the family, over the house. When I left, their spirits seemed to have been lifted in our time of prayer. After calling them the following morning, they were still holding on and doing better as a family, so I praised God for that.

Unfortunately, this kind of situation is not all that uncommon. When a sickness or misfortune can't be explained, the default assumption is that it was a witch doctor that cast a curse or one of the lwa (spirits) were upset with the individual or family. The Western concept of free will is almost non-existent in this context. People strive to appease the spirits around them so that no harm or sickness will befall them. Some refuse medical treatment in the belief that what is going on is purely spiritual.

Here is where two worlds collide: The Western tendency is to deny the reality of the spiritual realm. In doing so, everything is reduced to purely materialistic explanations - science. The other extreme, as exemplified by animistic cultures, is to explain everything through spirits and magic. The spirits dominate reality and humans must constantly fight to appease them in order to survive. Or through magic, people can control supernatural powers in order to achieve their desires. In the Western world, science deals with the empirical world and leaves religion to handle the other-worldly stuff. But as scientific knowledge expands, the need for religion decreases. There is a middle ground that includes both realities of the physical and the spiritual.

I was also reminded of Jesus' words in Luke 14:26. "If anyone comes to me and does not hate his own father and mother and wife and children and brothers and sisters, yes, and even his own life, he cannot be my disciple." Jesus' use of extremes paints a picture of what I had just witnessed. See, Herbie's cousin is an houngan – a witch doctor. He had already spoken with Herbie and told him that he could make her better. Herbie had refused, not wanting to forsake his trust in Jesus. To the rest of his family, it appeared that he hated his daughter. She was suffering; potentially dying! Yet he refused to act on an opportunity to make her better. Instead, he stood his ground as a believer. Though not all stories end this way, by the grace of God, Spendie did get better and two weeks later was back in school. Those that had placed their trust in the magic and mysticism of voodoo had to take a step back and acknowledge a higher power at work in this family's life. And his name is Jesus.

Kanaval

There is a holiday in Haiti known as "Kanaval" which coincides with Mardi Gras everywhere else. In Mardi Gras, people indulge the flesh right before the 40-day lent season of repentance and fasting. Kanaval is no different in essence, though it is heavily influenced by voodoo traditions and rituals. That typically means that voodoo and "mystic" activity increases during this time and continues to be at a heightened level up through Resurrection Sunday. Here in Haiti, the Lenten season—Ash Wednesday to Easter Sunday—is filled with Haitian voodoo ceremonies and practices. Particularly on Holy Week, the most significant of these is the *rara*. A quick Google search for "Haiti Carnival" shows this, among other things: "*Rara* is called "Vodou taken on the road" by Haitians. Processions of female dancers follow male Vodou religious leaders, accompanied by drummers and vaksen bands, stopping at crossroads, cemeteries, and the homes of community leaders. *Rara* rituals are public acknowledgements of the power of local "big men" in the communities. Money is given to the leaders of *rara* organizations and communities during processions. The incorporation of military costumes and dance steps in *rara* processions is also an acknowledgement of the community hierarchy, and the folk belief that Vodou rituals, including *rara*, supported the success of the Haitian Revolution, and the continued well-being of Haiti. *Rara* band members believe that they have made a contract with spirits, and must perform for seven years, otherwise adversity will result."

During the week of Kanaval, we heard some new sounds coming from the neighborhood. Now, it's typical for loud speakers to be doing political propaganda into all hours of the night. We experienced that leading up to the elections and even the inauguration. However, with all of that behind us, the loud speakers seemed oddly out of place. In the middle of the day, we'd hear bull horns, broadcasting people speaking, but we couldn't make out what they were saying. Last week, we were walking to another missionary's house and realized we were passing right next to where the speakers were located. When we asked the other missionary about it, he said it was a voodoo community that had recently sprung up in our neighborhood and they were (obviously) being very vocal.

Cathi commented later that when we were living in Chambrun, people would tell us all the time that the village was deep into voodoo and that it just wasn't that common in other places. Given Kanaval and the occurrences like this one in other communities, that is not the case. What was encouraging was that the missionary told us that several church leaders were getting together often to pray against this.

During this Kanaval season, much of the week is a national holiday, which means no work and no school. Many churches send their youth on retreat, hold outreach events, crusades, etc. I was invited to do a 3-day conference in Pernier, at a church atop the mountain village. We started on Sunday afternoon and finished at noon on Tuesday. During the three days, we took a deeper look into Scripture at what God has revealed about Himself for us and how that should impact our lives. In contrast to the bright lights, loud music, and colorful celebration of Mardi Gras, this was a very simple conference. But it was a great few days, digging into God's Word and worshiping together. They asked some tough questions as they genuinely wanted to grasp more of God. Our motto for the three days was that we didn't want to just fill our heads with knowledge but fill our hearts with a deeper appreciation for the God we serve and worship. This was also in stark contrast to the spirit of Kanaval which glorifies selfish desires. Instead, people were gathered to deny themselves and glorify the only One worthy of worship.

10 Ministry

Sunday, June 1, 2014 was my third Sunday in a row preaching. I typically preached on the third Sunday of each month, so that was as planned. The last Sunday in May, I had been invited to a small, young church in Onaville. However, this particular Sunday was a surprise. I found out I was preaching at around 8pm on Saturday evening!

I liked to take a full week to prepare for a sermon for a few reasons. First of all, Creole not being my native language, it took a little more effort to read and study for the purpose of putting a message together. I eventually could do this in Creole, rather than in English and then translating it over. Several times, early in my time here, I would write a sermon in English and then found there were difficulties in translating it to Creole. Sometimes meaning was lost because the reading in Scripture was rendered differently, for example. However, another main reason was that it gave me time throughout the week to find ways to communicate the message in a proper cultural context. Often times, that meant finding an illustration from everyday life that would communicate a spiritual truth. I might have been able to think of a good story or example off the top of my head that would help illustrate a certain point, but chances were that it would only help if I had been preaching to an American audience.

I believe it was November of last year when I preached a sermon on sanctification, which was the theme for the month. I described it as a process through which the Holy Spirit transforms us into what God desires us to be. During my preparations, I thought of a butterfly and the fact that it starts off as a caterpillar. That ugly creature goes into a chrysalis and comes out a butterfly, completely changed - a new creature. After I shared this information, I got blank stares. Now, every 6th grader in America takes science and learns about metamorphosis. Unfortunately, I did not take into account that 50% of my audience was illiterate and the highest level of education in that community was 6th grade. Very few, if any, people knew that a caterpillar and a butterfly are the same animal, at different stages. My illustrations and complimenting material needed to be better thought-out so that it actually communicated well to this particular culture.

The other consideration, due to the lack of education in that community was the complexity of the message. Studies that bounce from text to text were not practical - half of the people don't read, so they can't follow along. Likewise, sermons that were heavy in new knowledge were not often received well. Background information on the authors or original language studies, for example, while useful for me to get at the heart of a passage, were lost on that audience. What these people were hungry for was application. How can they make their lives relevant to what Scripture says? Some things are black and white, therefore, easy to make applicable. Others are dependent on the expressions of culture and require more thought and exploration.

In light of all that, you can get a feel for my stress levels on Saturday night, as I realized I had 12 hours to write a message that would communicate God's Word in way that was culturally relevant in both delivery and in application, so that it was understood and capable of leading people to action. I spent some time in prayer before even opening the Bible (which I had to look for, since I'd given mine away!). God knew what the congregation needed to hear. He also knew how I would default to prepare for the message in such a short time. The message was clear and simple, yet it moved people to action. The best preparation for ministry is done in the power of prayer.

Evangelism

In May of 2012, President Martelly inaugurated a new development of houses, named Village Lumane Casimir. They were an answer from the president to the IDP camps all over Haiti. In October of the following year, they "re-launched" the idea in the form of a grand opening for the village. Earlier that year, there were still few families living in the village. However, over the summer, there were a lot more moving there, which was only a mile and a half from the NVM campus. Casimir Village had electricity and running water, which was a huge step in housing here in Haiti. There was a school right in the middle of the village, they have their own police station, fire station, and it was said they provided transportation to Port au Prince to get to work and back.

One of the deacons at the church put together a small team to go on a door to door evangelism visit to the village. That's a misleading term, but it's probably the best way to describe it to an American so that they get the picture. However, you didn't really have to knock on any doors, because people were generally sitting outside on their "porch" interacting with everybody else. It doesn't matter if you're talking about a mud hut or a cinder block house - this is part of the Haitian culture. In this village, the porch area was around the back, where the kitchen and bathroom were situated. So, when the team got back, I told the deacon that if he went again anytime soon, to tell me and I would go with him. One morning, he walked into my office and said they were going at 4pm. I made sure I arranged my schedule to join them.

When 4pm rolled around, there were 12 people getting ready to go. There were also 4 church leaders present - Clerice (Children's Ministry Director), Faince (deacon), Malone (Music Director), and myself. We split up into four groups, each of us leading one. I had one of the girls from the Children's Home, Mitanya (13), and another young man, Oksiben. I drove us all out to the village in the tap-tap and we split up to go our separate ways.

I told Oksiben he could lead the way and initiate conversation, since I wasn't sure what would be culturally acceptable. Once I realized it didn't matter, when he engaged in conversation with one, I would go on to talk with the next person, whether at the next house or around the corner. At one point, Clerice (who is also fluent in English) called me over because he'd found a white man living there. I think we were both surprised to see another "blan" living in the area. Later, we came across two ladies talking on their porch, so Oksiben stopped to talk with them. They had both accepted Christ previously, so we gave them some tracts to share with others and were getting ready to move on, when I suddenly felt the urge to ask if I could pray for them. When I asked, one of the ladies asked if I wanted to pray for the kids upstairs. She ran an orphanage which had 14 kids living there, upstairs. I agreed and she led us upstairs. My heart was not prepared for what I saw.

Most of the kids could not move on their own. Four of them had hydrocephalus, where their heads were so enlarged, they could not lift them. Many of the kids just lay on the floor. Another woman was there bathing some of the children. I realized this is what a Haitian orphanage probably often looks like - kids who are unwanted, just dropped off or abandoned. I wondered what Mitanya was thinking as we walked in. I smiled at the kids as my heart broke, then prayed. I prayed for the kids, for the orphanage, and for these ladies that had a hard task before them. As we were leaving, I encouraged the other two to ask if the person we talk to wants prayer - you never know what they'll ask for prayer, and most of the time, they'll say yes.

As we continued walking the streets of Casimir Village, we asked everyone we talked to if they wanted us to pray, and I prayed for a lot of people and a lot of different things yesterday. Among those prayers, I had the privilege of leading two people in a prayer of repentance and surrender to Christ. One was a girl between 8 and 10 that Mitanya had begun talking to. The girl had been in church all her life, but never made a decision for herself. After I prayed with her, we gave her a New Testament, when she said she could read some. Immediately, she grabbed my hand and asked me to come with her. She wanted me to come pray for her mother. We walked a few houses down and came upon a woman sitting in a wheelchair and an older man who was blind. I took a deep breath, as I understood what this girl was really asking me. I sat in a chair they offered me (always humbling) and visited with them for a while. Afterwards, I told them that I was there because this girl, Jasmine, had asked me to come and pray with them. I asked if I could and they agreed. I didn't pray for physical healing - not because I didn't believe that it could happen, but because from the conversation, it was clear they needed emotional healing. After praying, I invited them to join us for church and gave them a number in case they needed transportation on Sunday morning.

The house I visited after this, I led a single mother of a toddler in a prayer of surrender to Christ as well. At this point, much of the team had caught up with us, so everyone began to pray out loud for this family. I looked over and the girl that I had prayed with not 30 minutes ago to accept Christ was standing there, praying for this family, too.

I drove everyone home after this and returned to my family. I was so exhausted on every level, I basically ate and went to bed. It wasn't until the following morning during my quiet time that I really processed the events of the visit to Village Lumane Casimir. I kept thinking of the simple principle that the eternal is more important than the temporal. Poverty is rampant in Haiti - one of poorest countries in the world. But if you look at the poor's definition of poverty, it has less to do with material possessions and more to do with physiological and social factors. They would use words like humiliation, fear, depression, isolation, powerlessness, low self-esteem, and shame. To put the eternal over the temporal is to recognize that Jesus can and will transcend poverty and meet people where they are and be the answer to their spiritual poverty. In Luke 15:1-7, we read the story of the lost sheep. More than any other seemingly important thing, what that sheep needs most is to be with its shepherd. It's so easy to see in a parable and yet, it also stares us in the face every day of our lives.

Life and Death

In December of 2015, I was invited to go to a mass wedding in Onaville. The date just happened to coincide with the day of the church anniversary celebration as well. This is a church that NVM planted in Onaville (largest tent city after the earthquake of 2010) and had grown considerably in the short three years it had been around. In preparing for the wedding, I helped Pastor Massillon with some of the logistics in getting wedding dresses and suits and rings for the couples. Several folks from the States helped us in that, which really made it a special day. Six of the couples were all married on December 7. We were supposed to start at 7:30 am, but started a bit late because one of the couples had not yet arrived! The couples were all decked out, looking great. The vows were those we are used to hearing (just in French/Creole). But there was a lot about the ceremony that was not what we were used to. First of all, the fact that it was six couples all being wed at the same time was rather different. As a result, there was no procession of any bridal party or the bride(s). There was no unity candle, no runner, no one giving the brides away. Yet, in a culture where it's ok for men to have multiple women, these couples vowing to love each other exclusively and making a commitment before the church and God was such a huge statement.

Though I wasn't expecting it, I was invited up after they had all said their vows and was asked to pray for them. They all knelt down, facing their new spouses, and bowed their heads as I had the privilege of praying that God would bless their marriages, families, and that they would be a light and example of God's faithfulness to others. Church lasted another few hours (until 12:30) and then came the reception! We were honored by being served goat meat, but there was chicken, beef, fish, rice, beets, and all sorts of other cultural delicacies. There was lots of food and people just enjoying fellowship together. It was truly a day of celebration!

Then, just days after this celebration, I got news that an older woman in our church had passed away. In fact, Carmène hadn't been at church that last Sunday due to illness when I was in Onaville. This little old lady was full of spunk. She was a short and tiny framed woman. Carmène was 74(ish) years old when she died, but she was energetic up to the end. I couldn't help but smile, seeing her dance her heart out every Sunday in worship. She was a sweet lady. She would always greet me after church with a big hug and kiss. I was asked to do the funeral that coming Friday. Having never done one in Haiti, I asked a lot of questions of cultural importance. The elements of the funeral were essentially the same. However, the way in which grief is expressed in this culture is a bit different from what we're used to in the States. It reminded me of studies of culture in biblical times. Jesus crashed several funerals where people were wailing inside and outside the house, with plenty of professional musicians to play loudly, etc. After the service, there was a processional march with the casket to the grave site. The church was not far from her house (which is where the tomb/sepulcher was). Along the way, others from the community joined the procession to the grave site. That paints the picture a little more accurately for this culture. Yet, the hurting is the same. People lost a mother, a sister, a friend. I preached a short sermon focusing on the fact that as believers, we do not mourn like those who have no hope. Perhaps due to the more "vocal" nature of this culture, it was obvious that there was indeed hope in the midst of the mourning.

Approaching two years in a new culture, there were a few observations that I had made. Sin's consequences bring grief and sorrow in any context. Death is a universal truth and proof of the fall. Yet other aspects of culture that are counter-biblical bring their own consequences as well. And they deprive people of joy and fullness. Jesus didn't just die for us to go to heaven when we die—he restored our relationship to God, which starts in the here and now! And the joy that comes from knowing Him is another aspect of life that crosses cultural boundaries. We have rejoiced with people through baptisms, in dedicating their children to God, in marriage, and in a number of other ways where God was being honored and glorified. Regardless of what the cultural customs and norms in any country, there is nothing that compares to knowing God and making Him known!

11 ENCOURAGEMENT

In May of 2014, I injured my knee. For those that know me well, this likely would not come as a surprise. It's probably less of a surprise that I was injured on the soccer field. What can I say? I love to be active and play sports and it's a great way to interact with people and bond with them. Cathi would like me to remember that I'm not as young as I used to be and that I don't heal as fast as I used to, either!

That year, we had a Haiti vs. USA game on the NVM campus. A visiting American medical team played against the Haitian staff here. It was actually the second annual game, since we had played a similar match just days after I had arrived in Haiti the year before. Each team was asking me to play with them. The Haitians said that since I had been living there for a year, I qualified to be on their team. The Americans of course said that I was still American, therefore I needed to play with them. In the end, I joined with the American team, because the Haitians didn't want to be told that their victory was invalid because of having a foreigner!

I played my heart out. With only one minute to go in the game, I collided with someone else and fell to the ground as my knee audibly popped, sending shooting pains throughout my leg. The initial thought was that I'd torn my ACL. As God would have it, there happened to be an orthopedic doctor in that very group. Dr. Marshall said that knees were his specialty. He operated on at least seven a week. He recommended surgery due to my active lifestyle. Though I could potentially wait to get it fixed, if there was other damage, I should do it sooner rather than later to avoid compounding issues. The first step was to get some images of the knee to see what the extent of injury was.

We did some looking around for an MRI to confirm the damage to the knee and found that there is only one machine in the whole country! After draining our Haitian bank account to pay for the images, we got the results that indicate there is damage elsewhere in the knee. More than a week after the incident, I still have a lot of swelling and though I wake up virtually pain free in the mornings, by the evening, there's a lot of discomfort. Additionally, I sent the report to the VA in the US (since I have service-connected disability for that knee already) and found that the orthopedic surgery had a wait list of 2 years.

I was open and honest when this initially happened that I was discouraged. Since then, it seemed like the hits wouldn't stop coming. My activities and normal routine were seriously limited due to mobility. The MRI ended up being quite a financial burden on the family. Additionally, there was the financial considerations of changing flights for surgery in the

US to either return early or leave later, to account for recovery time. That presented other issues of whether I would be alone for surgery or recovery or if my family would be displaced for that entire time... you get the idea.

What's interesting is that in this this dark time for me, God was still encouraging me. The day after the injury, I had several visitors from the Haitian staff. In the following days, people from the village came to wish me well. My friends from Onaville once again walked for hours to visit me too! Then, my friend Easy walked to Port-au-Prince to pick up the MRI results for me when I couldn't get off campus to do it myself. I'd been blessed by through these relationships in what, for me, had been one of my toughest times there.

Later that year, all the stress piled on and pushed me over the edge. The Christmas season of 2014 was one of the loneliest times in my life, following one of the hardest years of my life – the first full year on the mission field. Oh, I wasn't alone, necessarily. I was surrounded by my family – Cathi and the four kids. At the same time, I felt so completely removed from reality that I hardly knew how to function. (In retrospect, this is probably when I finally hit culture shock, among other things.) My journal entry for December 26, 2014 reads like this:

<<For some reason, this has been a really hard week. On top of missing family in light of the holidays, I'm also feeling nostalgic – to a bad degree, I think. I find myself longing to be back in our house in Oklahoma, doing the things we used to do: going to the movies around the holidays, visiting family

and friends, playing games, playing in the snow, etc. I spent more than an hour in the room playing the electric guitar to worship music. Cathi was wanting me to be done with that, I guess and asked how long I was going to lock myself up in my room. I know she doesn't realize what's going through my head and that playing the electric is my coping mechanism. But I guess also, thinking about going overseas to a different country and having less, being able to do less and all that it implies is finally hitting me – and it's awful timing. And then, on top of this (yes, there's more), all the nostalgia from earlier has brought up old memories – of when I was young and stupid. I've been remembering a lot of my past mistakes and unfortunately, dwelling on them. That's bringing me down as well. I just want to sit and sulk, but at the same time, I don't want to feel like this. We were supposed to leave for a getaway this weekend, but had to postpone. I was secretly hoping that would snap me out of it… "All I need is You… All I need is You, Lord. Is You…" Help me, Jesus.>>

Now, how in the world does a missionary get to this point? There were multiple factors going into this. Not one sole thing was driving me to what I consider a depression. Instead, it was a series of events, conditions, and attitudes that facilitated it. Physically, we had moved our family of six from our nice home in Lawton, Oklahoma to a house half the size in Chambrun, Haiti. This meant multiple adjustments. We traded central air for a single window unit. We traded restaurants and movie theaters for a shared kitchen and cafeteria in a tent. There was also the adjustment of living simply. The difference in language creates a different kind of stress. All day long, we hear a language with which we're unfamiliar. Our brains are constantly processing information and never get a break. At the end of the day, we would finally realize how mentally exhausted we were, just from the constant translation going on in our heads. We would go to the grocery store and the kids would ask for their favorite cereal. Well, sure, I thought – until I realized that it cost almost $10 for the box! A pound of butter was $8 and strawberries more than $12 for a little basket. And switching to mangoes and pineapples is not that big of a deal. But when you suddenly realize that your normal way of life is no longer tenable, you've just defined what true culture shock is. But it wasn't just this.

Those are just the normal stressors of changing culture, which we knew were going to pose some degree of challenge. Those are the difficulties everyone expects. However, the occupational challenges completely blindsided us on arrival to our missions assignment. I arrived in Haiti in May 2013 under the assumption that I would be the staff and outreach pastor. That meant being the spiritual shepherd to the American staff on the ground – which at the time of arrival was two other couples and three single females, in addition to my family of six – as well as managing a pastoral leadership development program for 30-40 indigenous pastors. Four days after my arrival, one of the couples informed us of their resignation and return to the US. Their departure necessitated someone else's assumption of their role. That someone was me. That role was to host American short-term missions teams. The harsh reality was that if I had known that was what I would be walking into, I never would have left Oklahoma. However, this was no surprise to God, who in His sovereignty, led me to Haiti first before dumping that on me. I remember upon our arrival to NVM, in our empty house, we sat down to pray in our living room. What the Holy Spirit led me to pray was that He would empower us to do whatever was needed here; that He would remove our expectations and use us in whatever way we were needed. It wasn't until a few days after that prayer that I understood its implications. I wasn't going to pack up my family and go back. We were choosing to submit to God's will – a choice that still needs to be made on a continual basis.

You might ask how in the world I could feel alone with a continuous flow of American short-term missionaries coming down. Let me put it to you this way: We were the hosts to guests in our "home" for 45 out of 52 weeks a year. Regardless of how much help they provide to our ministry and even to our family, they were still guests for whom we were responsible. They still created work for us to do. Most teams were well-intentioned and were sincere in their drive to help. I enjoyed seeing God working in people throughout the week and seeing them be challenged spiritually. I liked hearing how their experiences there helped shape their mindset of the mission field they had waiting for them at home. That's all wonderful stuff! Yet, in the midst of all that, there was often a lack of understanding that while they were in Haiti for one week, I lived there. They were ready to go 100 miles per hour into whatever project and wanted to go until they dropped. They woke up at 6am and were at it until they collapsed in their bunk at 10pm. Again, that's great. I just couldn't physically, mentally, or emotionally do that 45 weeks out of the year.

The new role I was jumping into stretched me beyond my innate abilities – to the credit of the One who placed me there. And by the time I wrote that journal entry, the American staff situation had changed drastically too. Shortly after the couple moved back to the US, one of the nurses moved as well. Six months later, the other couple returned to the States. Around the same time, another family joined the staff. While we looked forward to this change, it proved to be one of our biggest challenges on the mission field. Ironically, the number one cause of missionaries leaving the field early is other missionaries. We were close to becoming part of that statistic. Our two families did not get along at all. I was able to avoid and ignore most things. However, Cathi got roped up in some pretty heated situations that frustrated, drained, and discouraged her – which in turn, became a stressor for me as well.

I was discouraged, to say the least. When the "normal" difficulties and frustrations of living in a foreign country surfaced, it was surmounted by the fact that there were no sympathizers among us. There was no desire to have community. There was no desire to seek God together. As the supposed staff pastor, I felt like a failure in that regard. At the end of a long day in the hot sun, mentally weary from translating and solving emergent problems, I did not have the luxury of going to a peaceful home. After putting the kids to bed, we would sit on the couch and I would listen as Cathi verbally processed the frustrations of her day, the feelings that were hurt by the accusing stares, and the disdain with which she had been treated. The last of my energies of each day were spent on encouraging her, comforting her, and praying for her. Before you praise me for being a godly man in all of this, I have to confess that my prayer life was not where it needed to be. There were some weeks where I did not pick up my Bible or utter a personal prayer to God. When I did pick up my quiet time with the Lord again, this would often add to the stress with the guilt of being inconsistent with this.

In that particular season, I was also recovering from an injury and a resulting surgery. I was always an athlete growing up. In June 2014, I suffered a knee injury that required me to go back to the States to have surgery in July. I was forced to wait four months before I could run again. When I tried to run again in December, the pain and discomfort made me reconsider and wait six full months before running. I hated not being able to run. Running was a de-stressor. On top of all the stress piling on, one of my outlets for it was not a viable option.

There was no margin in our lives. You know what margin is. It's the area on your paper around the printed material. It's the buffer from the edge of the page. We use expressions like "margin of error" to refer to the allowable amount we could be off our calculations. However you want to describe it, we had none. The concept of a margin is that when you're writing a word that goes over the red line by a little bit, you've got some blank space there to catch the extra letters. Similarly speaking, when you're caused to stretch in an area of your life, there are reserves (margin) that allow you to muster up the strength, energy, or whatever in order to deal with it. Any one of the factors I mentioned would be manageable in light of having margin in life. Even things as complicated as adapting to a new culture can be handled well. We were crashing because we had no margin of any kind.

But on top of it all, I felt alone. There was no one I could turn to and no one who was checking up on me to see how I was doing. I was overworked and overstressed. It felt like someone had pushed me out the door of an airplane without a parachute and I had no idea how much time before I hit the ground. There's this flattering misconception of missionaries that actually hurts them. Somehow, missionaries are viewed as superhuman or at least superChristian to the point of not needing anyone else. The things that you strive for at your home church – community, fellowship, accountability – are often not accessible to the missionary. Everyone thinks they're somehow beyond those things. So they normally don't think to check up on them. At the same time, I didn't want to write about these things on my blog or in my newsletter or anything that may be read by my supporters for fear of losing their support. I didn't want someone reading about my struggles and say, "Well, then he shouldn't be on the mission field" and stop supporting me – whether through finances or prayer! So I got stuck in this box of isolation, nobody reaching out to me, and I was afraid of reaching out to anyone else. Revisiting my earlier question of how this happens to a missionary, I would say that it's simply a misunderstanding. There's a lack of understanding as to what missionaries face on the field. There's a lack of understanding as to what support missionaries need. There's a lack of understanding from the missionaries of what they need until they're experiencing it! But we think we shouldn't feel this way, so they hide it in shame and continue to drive themselves deeper into self-exile.

A little over a year after the Christmas journal entry, a small group from Dayspring came to visit us. Tim and Cindy Evans, our lead pastor and his wife along with Jamie Ball, a young woman who'd been on the worship team with us, came to stay for a week in Haiti. During this week, I was leading a 3-day conference for pastors in the area. Cathi was working with the kids in the school to update child sponsorship records. It was busier than average in that Cathi and I both had to work outside the home, which always was a challenge when homeschooling. Cindy stepped in to do the schooling with the kids that week as well as prepare dinners every night. Tim attended the seminars and helped with the behind the scenes stuff. He ran to fill pitchers of water, grab lunch and help serve the pastors. If there was something that had to be done in the middle of the conference, he'd get up and do it, so that everything could continue to run smoothly. During the course of the week, Cathi and I also had the opportunity to go on a date while the kids stayed with our guests.

They didn't come to Haiti to do a traditional short-term missions trip. They weren't expecting to go out and see the villages around us nor were they worried about experiencing the culture. We sure did some of those things as Cathi and I desired to share what our life entailed. We visited some of the pastors that I was mentoring and Tim and I prayed for them in their churches. We walked down to the village to visit our "Haitian family" so that they could meet them. We spent time with our five Haitian kiddos and kept up with our normal schedule and they got to be a part of it. In the evenings, we'd worship in music together after dinner as Cindy and Jamie did the dishes. We spent some time in prayer as a group. They sat and listened to our struggles and challenges, our hopes and dreams. Their agenda was to be an encouragement. And it was exactly what we needed. At the end of that week, we felt refreshed, recharged, and ready to keep going.

12 TRANSITIONING AGAIN

After living on the NVM campus for three and half years, we moved to a house (not far) off campus, in the community. As we transitioned, I couldn't help but remember the transition from the US to Haiti. We were selling what we had, fundraising, learning a new language, and preparing to go overseas. There was some anxiety over leaving behind the familiar for the unknown, but also a lot of excitement for the realization of the mission for which God had called us. All those anxieties were appeased as we learned the language, learned some of the culture, made friends, and began figuring out what ministry looked like in this context. It isn't unlike that at all this time around. We left behind the familiarity of living on campus, with security, 24-hour electricity (most of the time), running water, and other expats as neighbors. Instead, we moved into a house where electricity was supposed to be on half the time, but we realistically got it at most eight hours a day – and which eight hours was anybody's guess! During that time of power, a water pump filled our storage water tank on our roof, so that we had water during the times of no power. When that ran out, we could go to the well directly and pump water out for what we needed. Simple tasks, like doing laundry, couldn't even be planned anymore, but were more of a reaction to the accessibility of power and water. When the time allowed, we washed by hand, so that we could get by, but if we did everything by hand and went to the market every day to get our food, all our time would have been consumed in those things, rather than allowing us to do ministry. Just as before, we were figuring out a new normal; trying to get into a new rhythm of life.

We were fortunate enough to have found a house large enough (and affordable) to accommodate our family, plus have extra space to have guests and even groups come visit and work with us here. What that meant was that we were primarily occupying the upstairs of this new house, so that we could later use the downstairs as the hosting space. The stairs leading up to that second floor was very narrow and not conducive to carrying pieces of furniture… or a fridge… or a stove up them. However, we had a nice balcony from that second floor. On moving day, we backed up the truck to that balcony and literally lifted everything straight from the truck up onto the balcony to carry into the upstairs. No ramp, no problem! I sat on the ledge of the balcony, bending down and hoisting things up. My body reminded me later that I'm not as young as I used to be, though. It was quite a different moving experience!

One of the things we noticed is that relationships seemed to be easier in that context. Where people (locals) used to be apprehensive of visiting us on campus, we had people stop by all the time to see us at our new house. This was exactly one of the things we were hoping for to give us the opportunity to become even more immersed in the culture. We didn't know all that God had planned for us in that season. But we can look back on the previous one with gratefulness at all that we learned, all that we experienced, and all the ways that God showed us His provision, protection, and guidance. It was clear He was calling us to a different chapter in our ministry here in Haiti, so we jumped forward, knowing He'd already taken care of the anticipated challenges and using the difficulties to continue to mold us in the image of His Son, Jesus. To Him be the glory.

New Connections

One of the things we were able to do in the downstairs "hosting" space was to hold a Bible study for expats – other English-speaking missionaries. We were able to provide a place for them to come and be edified, encouraged, and worship with others in their own heart language. I know we had underestimated the importance of that over the years we were in Haiti. There is something about being able to sing, pray, and study the word in your native tongue that is more fulfilling than doing all of that in a foreign tongue, where you're continually translating and trying to make sense of it all. Even after you become fluent in that language, there is still a greater edification that takes place in your heart language.

As we put out notice that we wanted to host something like

this, missionaries popped out of the woods. We started meeting other couples doing extraordinary things in Haiti that we would have never otherwise met. The folks from NVM still came down the street to join us. But we also had people come from across the bridge in Clercine and Tabarre, down by the airport to our house. There were some other missionaries that didn't live too far but had no idea they were there. We started to build long-lasting friendships with them and were mutually encouraged by our involvement in each other's lives.

Teaching Ministry

One of the major reasons for this transition was the conviction that I was to be engaging more in a teaching and discipleship ministry. At Nehemiah Vision Ministries, I was running the Pastoral Development Program which consisted of doing a seminar every last Saturday of the month. There were around a hundred pastors and church leaders that came. We would cover topics like biblical study, Christian leadership, and anything else that would help these men in their perspective ministries. After a couple of years, I developed some strong relationships with a select few from the whole group. Some of these developed into meaningful mentorships where I had the privilege of speaking into their lives.

But this was far from my focus. I had other responsibilities at NVM. As I mentioned previously, the first of these was to be the Missions Director. I was in charge of the short-term missions team program at the ministry. NVM saw over 600 people per year stay on their campus to do different projects and tasks in order to help the overall progress and vision. Some of these were construction projects, some came to do VBS, others still to run mobile medical clinics, while others helped me run pastoral conferences. There were plenty of options for teams to engage in ministry in partnership with NVM. Truth be told, this is not what I had come to NVM to do. I had moved there to be the staff and outreach pastor. However, the folks that had run the short-term missions program left the same year we arrived and Cathi and I found ourselves in their shoes. What was supposed to be a temporary position until they found someone else turned into a position of more than three years.

God increased my passion for teaching and mentoring. I asked several times if I could expand the pastoral development program but was turned down. Nehemiah Vision Ministries' focus was social justice work. In fact, the founder, Pastor Pierre, was also the national director for Campus Crusade for Christ. He would often say that Nehemiah Vision Ministries was the social arm of the spiritual vision cast by CRU. In that light, NVM was not keen on expanding that program. And that's not a bad thing. Ministries have to be clear and focused in order to be effective. This venture happened to be outside the scope of NVM's focus. So, I sought other opportunities to be involved in that.

In August of 2016, I had the opportunity to teach with Training Leaders International in Haiti at a school in Croix des Bouquets. The school, a Bible institute, was partnering with TLI to supplement their curriculum in developing church leaders. During the two weeks I taught students with TLI, I had the opportunity of speaking with the school's director, Pastor Jean Garry Auguste. He had a Masters' degree in Christian Education and started the school in order to raise up more educated church leaders in Haiti. The school had two programs spanning two years. The first year earned students a certificate in theological studies and the second year led to a diploma which allowed students to seek ordination with their perspective churches. The challenge the school had was that the school could not run both programs simultaneously. They only had three staff members. As a result, they would run the certificate program only for 3 or 4 years. Then, they would run the diploma program for one year, inviting back all the students from the previous years' certificate program while putting the certificate program on hold. In my conversations with Pastor Garry, I found that they didn't have the funding to increase staff, but without more staff, they would never have the funds to expand their program. I asked him if having a volunteer teacher would help them accomplish this. After thinking about it for a while, he said it would. I went home and prayed about this and decided to offer my services to Institut Biblique de la Croix des Bouquets (IBC).

Pastor Garry was elated and asked if I could start that fall. In October 2016, I started teaching Old Testament Survey for the certificate students and Christian Leadership for the diploma program. Later that year, TLI returned to Haiti and I taught a Hermeneutics course with them at the school. In December of 2016, we moved off the NVM campus so that I could engage in this and continue doing seminars in partnership with other churches in rural areas.

Pastor Garry also had a heart for families. To this end, he ran a marriage enrichment group that met several times a year. In early 2017, he invited Cathi and me to give a seminar on marriage at their next get-together in February. We were so excited for the opportunity for this! Cathi and I love doing ministry together and we welcome the opportunity to engage in this way. Additionally, we are so grateful for the years of marriage we've enjoyed. We certainly don't have everything figured out, but God has allowed us to experience a lot in a relatively short amount of time. From military deployments, multiple children, many moves, and many more events that have drawn us closer together and tested our resolve to glorify God in the midst of our relationship. This seminar was not our last. We eventually did another marriage seminar for an organization called Haiti Design Co. We were honored to share our story of God's love and grace manifested through us in our commitment to each other.

EVM

One of the things we suspected in making the move from Nehemiah Vision Ministries was the loss of some support. There were some donors that supported us financially primarily because we were affiliated with NVM. They had a vested relationship with the organization and were happy to financially back us as we worked for the organization they supported. We started making the calls and letters to our donors and our suspicions proved true as a few major donors said they would finish their contributions when our time with NVM was done.

Shortly thereafter, I received a call from another organization that had previously partnered with NVM and with whom I was familiar. Ezra Vision Ministries was born our of an initial partnership with Nehemiah Vision Ministries. Just as in the biblical account, Nehemiah and Ezra both worked toward the rebuilding and reestablishment of Jerusalem after the exile, EVM rose up to be a support to NVM's efforts in the rebuilding of Haiti. Specifically, Ezra wanted to focus on furthering education. The founder of Ezra Vision Ministries, Ronnie Hawkins, was a general in the Air Force when he started the ministry and had since retired when he made the phone call to me. I had (and still have) a great deal of respect for this man. Ronnie told me that he would love to have my help as a chief of staff of the efforts in Haiti for which they were willing to compensate me. He even told me to name what I wanted my hours and my salary to be!

Ronnie and I would have many conversations afterward, but I accepted the position as Haiti Chief of Staff for Ezra Vision Ministries. Since their days partnering with NVM, they had founded a school in Onaville. The school director was a good friend and already ministry partner of mine. Pastor Massillon had hosted several pastors' conferences that I had done in Onaville, as well as the officiator of the mass wedding I had attended. In this new partnership, God provided the finances we would need, as well as provided more ministry partners who would further the discipleship efforts he had already prompted me to start.

13 PARENTING ON THE MISSION FIELD

The following are blogs Cathi wrote on parenting in Haiti:

Sometimes it is a simple question, like "Where are you guys from?" Other times it is the obvious moment when your 7-year old still won't eat with utensils, because none of his friends eat with a spoon or fork. And then there are the even more obvious moments when he carries a bowling ball on his head when his aunt takes him bowling "for the first time" because he could not remember what bowling is. And why wouldn't he carry the ball on his head? Everything is carried on the head in Haiti, and it really improves posture and allows you to carry even more weight...this is his world.

Each of these moments make us chuckle, but they tell a much deeper story. While enjoying a day at the beach in Haiti, a gentleman struck up conversation with our family. The very typical first question was, "Where are you from?" Our youngest paused and then replied, "I don't remember where I am from." Our friend explained that she is from Oklahoma, and then informed the gentleman that we live here in Haiti. Without missing a beat our youngest said, "Oh yea! I've been to Oklahoma before!" We all chuckled and reminded him that is where we lived - and he was born - before moving to Haiti.

In the moment I handle these moments pretty well - at least I feel like I do. But later they come rushing back to me and I think through all the blogs and books I keep reading (or have on my to-read list) about third-culture kids (TCKs). Our youngest was just 4 when we moved to Haiti, so he will adopt more of the TCK posture than our older kids. Reflecting on this moment though - the moment of not remembering where he was from - I had to surrender it to God. American culture says so much about the foundation we give our kids, putting down our roots, and them knowing where they come from. All the parenting books I read before missions were completely focused on life in America. I often find myself out of my element and the enemy knows just where to attack. He likes to take these simple moments and innocent conversations and use them to tell me that I am a failure; surely I must be ruining my children. Yet, I look at the photo below and see a fun-loving, enjoyable young boy who loves life. So I cry out to God once again and ask that He guide us in this often lonely road of raising children on mission in a developing world.

So, when you find that your child cannot remember where he is from, or eats with his hands when clearly he is old enough to remember a utensil, focus on this: are you teaching them to "act justly, love mercy, and walk humbly with our God?

(Micah 6:8)" Because in the end, that is what God requires of us...that we live in this way, and that we teach our children to do the same (Deut. 6). So, let go of the little things, don't give the enemy any foothold, and keep on pointing your children back to the One who holds them closer than you imagine.

Expectations

"Don't touch your face!"

"You can't play in the dirt!"

"No running in the village!"

"Please don't share your water!"

These are phrases that we have consistently said to our children. None of these are things we ever thought we would say - definitely not with the frequency we now say them. My six-year old is a typical boy and he loves to run and play in the dirt. He has probably scared more than his fair-share of women in the community by running around and playing in the dirt. He simply does not understand their concern. They see a boy running and their memory jumps back to some child who ran and fell, and the scratch got terribly infected, causing amputation or worse - death. They see a child playing in the dirt and remember a young child who played in the dirt and ended up with a serious infection or worms - perhaps this too resulted in death in the story that replays in their minds.

Parenting on the mission field just is not the same as

parenting in your passport culture. You have to adapt to your surroundings, learn new cultural "no-no's," keep kids safe from totally new things that are often just as foreign to the parent! While you work to raise respectful young adults, you suddenly find yourself balancing and teetering between two worlds. It seems your family is always one step away from offending someone.

It is in these moments that you start to observe how others parent their children. Maybe you are blessed with a more experienced "veteran" missionary family to watch and model. Maybe you have met an incredible family on the mission field in your new home culture, and you can learn from them what is acceptable or not. Maybe you're pulling your hair out because you feel completely lost in this adventure and it is not quite what you imagined it would be. Praise God for His grace!

I remember in our first months in Haiti that I would change my responses to my children to match what the culture did. I realized this was not productive, as my kids did not know what was expected of them. We began to have lots of conversations about what is acceptable in each culture. Our kids will one day be masters at fitting into the crowd anywhere they go, because they can assess the situation and adapt to what is expected of them in order to avoid cultural mishaps. I pray that God uses this for His glory one day! Parents - it does not matter where you are raising your children - do not underestimate the importance of talking with them and sharing with them what your expectations are and why! If you do not have a good reason, you may want to re-think your expectations.

If you are at the beginning of your adventure, trust in God's Word! His Word will guide you, even if you have nobody else around you to tell you what to do.

- Teach your children to love unconditionally, to be gracious and kind, to care about and for others, to respect their elders, and to listen well.
- Teach your children to pray about everything, without ceasing.
- Teach them to follow your example by being a good enough example for them to follow!
- Teach your children to seek God's will first in their lives by modeling it for them, even on the hardest days.
- Lastly - but definitely not least! - teach your children to be humble and ask forgiveness when they blunder, because they most definitely will.

Raising your children in a foreign culture is not an easy task, but God is faithful and will equip you. He will walk with you as you try to guide your children closer to Him. This, my friends, is what parenting is all about.

14 GRACIA KIDS

Between Christmas and New Year's of 2014, Cathi and I went into the village of Rampa, which is in the opposite direction as Chambrun, but only a little farther. We went to visit a lady of the church, Silianis, who hadn't come to church in a little bit and we wanted to check up on her. She was the single mother of seven kids, one of whom was a special needs boy. Her jogging stroller that she used to push Johnny to church had broken, so she was forced to carry him if she wanted to get to church. She had done this several times and as a result, her back was hurting (as Johnny was then 5 years old) and was taking it easy. While we sat and visited with her and her kids, several other kids came from next door to her place to see "the blans." The kids had the tell-tale signs of malnutrition - some with swollen bellies, discolored hair, etc. Silianis then told us who these kids were.

That Christmas Eve, a mother took her five children, ages 9, 7, twin 4 year olds, and 3, to Onaville in the mountain and left them there. No one had heard or seen this woman since.

All five children were malnourished and looked smaller than their ages. The three year old had never been able to walk due to severe malnourishment. The older four kids actually walked all night to find their way back to their own village. The three-year-old was heard crying in the morning by someone walking by and was brought back to the village. I cannot state how much of a miracle all of this already was. Cathi saw the youngest girl, Rose Samelle (or just Rose), in the malnutrition clinic in November 2012 when we came to NVM to interview. She had captured Cathi's heart even then. When we heard that she had been dropped from that program, we believed she would not make it. Yet, here she was, alive.

Unfortunately, the mother of these kids destroyed a lot of relationships within this community and her family that there is no desire to care for the kids. There was an aunt that lives nearby who decided to try to look after the kids. Solanj (the aunt) was 65 at this time. She was deeply involved in voodoo - so much so that she was considered to be married to the spirit inside a tree. Years ago, one of her other children died and she assumed care for those five grandchildren. They were teens and in school, so she did her best to put a roof over their heads, feed them, and put them through school. Now, she had added these younger five to the number of kids she was responsible for. There was not adequate space for the kids, nor did she have the means to feed them all, let alone put them through school. They slept in a mud hut on the dirt floor, because there was no room for a second bed in it - Solanj (understandably) slept in the only bed in there. They didn't eat every day - sometimes going without food for two or three days at a time. While we had witnessed abject poverty in Haiti, God had allowed us to be absolutely broken for these kids.

We felt God asking us to jump into the situation and help in whatever way possible. We started by gathering some clothes for the kids and bringing sandwiches and other easy foods to carry. Then, we asked permission if we could bring the kids to church. Sunday mornings, we would go early to bathe the kids, get them dressed in nice clothes, and bring them on campus. There, they could have breakfast, go to church with us, then be fed lunch, then have an opportunity to just play with our kids for the afternoon before we feed them again and take them back to the village. Over the years of doing this, these Sundays became really special - chaotic mind you, but great. During the week, we would go down to Rampa every other day to either bring sandwiches or to bring them back here so that they could have the opportunity eat. Sometimes, the long walk and resulted in Cathi and I each carrying one of the kids! But in the first month that we invested in these kids, we saw them open up and their personalities come out. Makenson, the oldest, and I played soccer with a balloon one Sunday all afternoon. Miraline, though quiet and reserved, was playing with our girls' dolls, showing a tenderhearted nature. Dieuvelda, always serious, was spinning in her new dress, smiling and giggling up a storm. Dieuvelson, her twin brother, eats slower than his siblings and is always willing to share his food with them. Though quiet around other people, as soon as he was with us, he would start talking non-stop! And Rose began lifting herself up and walking while holding onto furniture. Though people in the village were convinced she couldn't talk, we started to hear her say phrases here and there to convey her feelings ("Give me water!"). Seeing all of this develop in them was a blessing in itself.

As we continued developing those relationships, our sending church stepped in to support as well. They asked what the kids' greatest need was at that point. Given the housing situation, we felt the kids would do better in school and have more security in their own future by having their own home, instead of bouncing around from house to house or sleeping on floors. Dayspring did a fundraiser that Christmas and came up with the money to provide the kids with a house. In the meantime, the local Haitian church decided to stand by our efforts as well in supporting the same kids. They began to provide boxes of rice to supplement their food and nutrition. Makenson would go to one of the church's deacons every other week and get a box of rice to take back to the house. Back on the housing front, there were some land issues to figure out which delayed the project. Once that got figured out, the house went up fairly quickly (as quick as things in Haiti go, anyway). Two weeks before the house was to be dedicated by the local church and prayed over, Solanj spoke with someone of the church. She said that she was tired of doing it all alone and how hard life was. In seeing all the love poured out by the Church, she realized she didn't need to. She surrendered her life to Christ in that moment. She even requested that the church prayer team come out to her house that next Tuesday to pray. They went into the house, grabbed anything that was still in some way linked to voodoo, and burned it all. This included the branches from the tree that contained the evil spirits to which she was joined. The support of the church to these kids and family made all the difference in the world. The love, grace, mercy, and kindness of God was poured out in such a tangible way that made Christ irresistible.

About a year later, a sixth child was dropped off at the house. The kids' sister, Mirlanda had been with her father all this time. However, he made plans to go to Chile (along with many Haitians looking for work), so he dropped her off with Solanj to be reunited with her siblings. Though she didn't have the same issues of malnutrition, she had also never been to school a day in her life. Eventually, all of the Gracia kids were enrolled in school, where they would be fed a meal each day and allowed the opportunity to get an education for their future.

The following is from Cathi's blog in December 2017:

We enjoyed celebrating Mirlanda's birthday in November. Mirlanda had never been able to celebrate her birthday - this was the first time she even really knew that it was her birthday. Out of all the Gracia children that we help with, Mirlanda is the "newest" to our family. She had lived with a godparent until this last summer. Thus, we have only gotten to know her since September when we returned from furlough. She is a sweet, quiet girl.

In preparing for Mirlanda's birthday, I asked her what she wanted. In Haiti, this question always refers to food. Since I usually make spaghetti on Sunday after church, she asked for rice instead. I asked if she wanted beans in the rice. "Yes," she said.

"And sauce, do you want sauce to go on the rice?" (a Haitian staple).

"Yes," she said.

That was it...I asked her what else she wanted and she stopped there. I asked if she wanted juice or pop, and she said juice. When I asked what kind, she gave me a brand name instead of a flavor.

I asked about dessert, and we agreed on a chocolate cake (brownies) like I had made for another recent birthday, after I suggested it. As I asked her about her birthday meal, I was struck by how little she asked for. When I ask my own children what they want, they can give me a menu for the day - sometimes even down to the snacks! Yet, Mirlanda could only think in terms of rice versus spaghetti.

This being her first birthday celebration, I realized that she had no idea what the limits were, or where she could begin. She could not even fathom what a feast she could ask for. She had never been asked what type of juice she wanted, so all that she knew was the brand. She did not even know she could ask for a specific flavor. This reminded me of the Scripture in Ephesians 3:20, "to him who is able to do immeasurably more than all we ask or imagine..."

Mirlanda was not able to fathom more than the rice because she had no way to gauge what was available. She had no experience to draw from, no wealth of menu options to think through. She had no idea what all we would have given her for her very first time celebrating her birthday. While maybe we would not have given everything she asked for, had she asked for a buffet line, she could not even begin to imagine what the options were.

We are the same way with God - we cannot begin to imagine the options of what we can ask Him for and all that He is willing to do for us. Over time, we begin to comprehend more of what is available, but we are always learning and never fully comprehend. His love for us is so much more than my love for Mirlanda. He sees perfectly, where I still see through my flawed perspective. He wants the best for us, whereas I can't even always see what the best is for all the kids I am trying to disciple. He tells us to ask for absolutely anything, and we don't even know that there are "flavors of juice" - we are still so basic in our thinking. I truly believe He looks at us, smiles, and says, "My child, if you only knew what all I would give to you." If He gave us His Son, why do we ever doubt that He would give us any good thing? What more could He give after His Son's sacrificial death?

We ended up taking Mirlanda and her siblings along with our family to a restaurant to celebrate. The restaurant has good rice with sauce, and fried chicken. Meat is a rare treat for these kiddos, so Mirlanda was pretty excited! She got the biggest piece. For dessert, we ended up getting ice cream instead of cake. It was the first time any of the Gracia kiddos had ice cream. They were all sold! We will need to do that again sometime soon, as it was probably the best part of their day.

In the end, we gave more than what Mirlanda asked for. I am so grateful that our God does the same. He is gracious to see what we need, and give it when we do not even have a clue. He hears our requests, and gives us SO much more. He is such a good God. I am so thankful that He continues to use "the least of these" - little children - to teach me about who He is and the love He has for me. May I start to imagine a little more of what He can and will do, and have the boldness to ask Him!

The More The Merrier

In 2017, we had the opportunity to return to the States for four months of furlough. In reality, we would be doing a lot of fundraising and travelling to update our supporting churches, but there would be downtime as well to get refreshed. We started in Michigan, where a lot of Cathi's family lives. Then we travelled to the Chicago area to visit some support churches. We made the drive to Oklahoma to visit Dayspring and later to Texas to visit a church we'd never been to before. On top of that, we had family now in Georgia and North Carolina, so we made a trek out there. While on the road, we decided to visit Washington, DC, New York, and Boston to get some historic sight-seeing in. It was great fun to do as a family.

During our second time in Oklahoma, while we were staying at some of our best friends' house, we realized Cathi was late on her monthly cycle. After Isaac was born in 2009, I had gone under the knife and gotten a vasectomy. I had gotten all the post-procedure checks to verify that I was sterile as well.

Naturally, we began to think of things like stress or maybe even sickness as possibilities for Cathi. At the same time, we figured it would be good to rule anything out that we could easily check ourselves. So, I ran to the pharmacy and picked up a simply home pregnancy test and brought it back to the house. As the lines marking positive clearly appeared on the test, we were in complete shock, to say the least. We were going to be new parents again after nine years…

We wrestled with the news. In part, it was difficult because we had our own selfish plans of early retirement when the kids were grown. We had kids young, therefore we would be "free" at an earlier age as well. But we also struggled because we didn't know what this meant for our ministry in Haiti. Was this God's way of telling us we were done? At first, that is what we thought, but as we actually sought God in prayer, we felt he was telling us we were not done in Haiti. Though this would be the beginning of the end, we made plans to return to Haiti.

One of the complications that this posed was Cathi's role in our ministry in Haiti. She travelled a lot to the villages to visit women and children to encourage and do life with. That wasn't going to be possible with an infant. In fact, the last year in Haiti, Cathi was mainly at home taking care of Miraya. In February 2018, we made preparations for Cathi to fly to the US yet again with our four children while I stayed in Haiti. She was in her third trimester at that point and due in mid-April. I would join them in April for the baby's birth and return to Haiti again for ministry, then go back again when they were all ready to come back to Haiti. It wasn't ideal, but especially after being gone for four months in 2017, I didn't feel comfortable leaving for another four months in 2018.

The Sunday before Cathi and the kids were to fly out, we were called up to the front of the church to be prayed over as a family. As we made our way back to our seats, I noticed Yola sitting in the congregation. Yola was the Gracia kids' mom. We had heard that she was back in town after years of being absent. People weren't sure what her motives were or what she was up to. Some suspected that she was pregnant again or something else was up. As we sat down, Pastor Pierre called her up to the front, telling the story of how this past week, she had surrendered to Jesus and now seeking to be submitted to his will for her life. Cathi and I were floored. Tears of joy welled up in our eyes as she walked to the front to give her testimony. Then, Pastor Pierre called me up to the front to pray for her in her new walk with Christ. I was so honored to pray for her in that moment. As our ministry in Haiti would change and our involvement in the Gracia kids' lives had to change, God had already been paving the way for that little family to be restored, beginning with Yola's relationship with him.

Return to Haiti

Blog from Cathi in June 2018:

Each time we return to Haiti, the transition has looked a little different. There have been times we have returned completely exhausted and ready to be back in our home. There are times we have come back with heavy hearts, sad to leave the states, and wondering what the next season would look like. This time was probably the hardest re-entry I (Cathi) have ever had. I really did not foresee how difficult it would be.

The first thing that made this so difficult was getting sick upon re-entry. However, I think another major contributing factor was that we spent 4 months in one place, in one home, in the states. We lived with "family," and got reconnected at our home church. The kids attended youth for the entire 4 months, and I attended a small group. We built new relationships and strengthened old relationships. We were really at home, and we were able to just figure out life there for that time frame.

After four months of that, it was hard to leave. We love our church and the many we call family there. We are so thankful for how well the church loves us and our kids. Leaving that, coming back to a place that often feels lonely and leaves us feeling disconnected from our state-side life, was hard. It took (and still takes) a lot of prayer daily – often minute by minute – to keep my attitude in check. There were times I cried and just wanted to go back. Yet, God would whisper to me once again that He has me in His hand, and I am right where I need to be. I may not understand the restrictions I feel on my free-flying spirit (routine and schedules are really not my thing, haha), and I am definitely grieving. I am grieving what I have lost back in Oklahoma – again. I am grieving what I have lost here in Haiti. I am not free to just go and visit with the women whom I love sitting and talking with. I cannot just jump in the car and go run errands for a day, or go out with a group of missionary women. I have a little one who needs me – every 3 hours at the very least. So, I am working on contentment.

So, for those who wonder, here are the top 10 things we are missing (other than the obvious – people), but we are choosing contentment without:

- Carpet – anything soft to stand on really!
- Hot showers with good water pressure
- A/C on demand
- Easy laundry: washing without a generator, and having a dryer
- No dust!
- Braum's ice cream
- Pandora
- Having a store within 10 minutes
- Ability to go out and take a walk, or ride bikes
- Fitting in

I have often seen a piece of artwork at the local metal market that says, "I am satisfied." It is a beautiful piece that I have never even considered purchasing, because it is a hard statement. Could I honestly hang this in my home? Lately, I think it is time to make this declaration – to remind myself daily, minute by minute, to be satisfied in Him and all He provides.

15 DISCIPLESHIP

Before I had left Nehemiah Vision Ministries, I had been approached by a young pastor, Jean Thenor. He had been going to the pastoral development seminars every last Saturday of the month and he desired to learn more. Admittedly, the first time he asked if he could meet with me in private, I was skeptical. I fully expected a long speech about what kind of ministry he was engaged in and how I could contribute financially to expand what that ministry was doing. He wasn't that way at all. Pastor Thenor was very humble. The first conversation was actually a series of questions concerning what he could do to learn more. I was impressed and could see that he was genuinely desiring to be mentored and discipled. We agreed to meet once a week and discuss different things, talk about life in general, and pray together. It felt a lot like the relationships I'd been in from his side. Three years later, these meetings were still going on.

A year after I met Thenor, I became the godfather to his second daughter, Neyemi. Then, when we prepared to go on furlough in 2017, Thenor and his family were going through a rough patch. I invited them to come live in the downstairs of our house. We certainly had the space and it was a mutually benefitting situation. They had six months to get back on their feet while we had someone watching our house during our time in the States. During the time that we overlapped, we certainly did life together as he got to see how we parent and relate to one another in the family. This was another level of discipleship as it was far more personal than just meeting once a week.

Pastor Thenor had also invited me to go to his church to do a seminar. As we discussed the possibility, he wanted me to do a whole series for a year at the church. His church was in the village of his wife's family. She had grown up there and they wanted to still have ties to the area. Thenor was the assistant pastor at the small church in the mountain. So, for one year, I travelled up the mountain about once a month in order to do a series on discipleship. The church ate it up, but even more than that, Pastor Thenor was learning a lot. From this series grew more opportunities for me to travel to other rural villages to do seminars and conferences. I tried to take Thenor with me to as many of them as I could. After some time, I started having him teach part of the material. Eventually, he was teaching the majority of it and I was simply going for moral support!

Later, I was approached by a few different people regarding more intentional discipleship material. Specifically, there was a mixed couple (Haitian man with American wife) who came to our Thursday night Bible study. Courtney had started an organization called Ansanm ("together") and their purpose was to reunite families that had been separated due to kids being placed in orphanages. They wanted to come alongside the parents and help them get on their feet to the point of being able to support themselves and care for their kids. At the same time, they wanted to make sure they were doing it all on a platform of discipleship. I was honored that they'd asked me to take part in this way. I partnered with them to write the curriculum, then train their staff. We hosted the training at our house, so Cathi hosted and enjoyed being part of the discussions as well. Even in the smallest ways possible, we have always enjoyed working together as much as possible. This was no different.

After I finished this training, I still had this curriculum that I'd developed. In short, the material focused on making disciples that make other disciples. It was intended to be as reproducible as possible, so that it could be put in motion with multiplying effects. God placed a desire in me to see this implemented in our own community. While I was in the States for Miraya's birth, I began praying about how to do this. This led to asking another friend, MacKendy, to host a small group at his house for 12 weeks to run through this program. Again, the intent was for them to take the material and concept to reproduce it in other groups.

I asked MacKendy to pick me up from the airport when I came back on my own to Haiti. On our ride back to my house, I pitched my idea. He was more than thrilled as he said he was praying about asking me to mentor him, teach him, and help him do more in the community. Once again, God exceeded all of our expectations as he orchestrated his will be done in us, before we even had a clue.

After my family returned to Haiti, we started up the study with two other couples. MacKendy and his wife Tasheena, Thenor and Farrah, and Vanqueur and Nadine. Cathi came with me on as many Monday nights as was possible. There was something special about our four couples getting together to dig into the word and pray together. Though I was teaching the material, I had asked MacKendy to lead everything else. Some weeks we would sing before we started and MacKendy would also close our time by praying for all of us. I was excited to think of what God could continue to do through each of those families there.

Pastor Thenor took furious notes and then asked me for a copy of the material. He went on to lead a group of 22 young men, using this program. The goal he set in doing this program was to prepare the men to take what they learn back to rural areas that don't have access to Bible schools or biblical training. These young men would be equipped to evangelize, and to defend their faith, making more disciples as they go.

Additionally, Pastor Thenor had an idea to get the teaching on discipleship recorded for audio playback. He told me that even though people will know that it is a foreigner, Haitians are hungry for this depth of information. For so long, biblical training (down to the basics of faith) has been reserved only for those wealthy enough or called to ministry (and in an area with access to the training). Part of the thought behind this material is to put the building blocks of Christian faith into the hands of anyone who wants it, free of charge. So, I set about recording the sessions one by one on my phone. There was nothing fancy about it. I sent them all to Pastor Thenor via WhatsApp, and Pastor Thenor has been forwarding them along since then.

Not long after, Pastor Thenor had two women visiting from France. They were born in Haiti but lived their adult years in France. They supported a church deep in the mountains; it was a 45-minute hike to the village. Pastor Thenor is connected with this church because he began mentoring the pastor there, in much the same way I mentored him. The women wanted to see how things are progressing. When they met me, they were astounded and very happy to meet the man who they'd been listening to. They had received the discipleship recordings and were so thankful for them. We stood humbled that God would reach people in France with this! Pastor Thenor continued to take over the teaching ministry I had started with him and expanding it to levels I could never have hoped to reach.

16 YET ANOTHER TRANSITION

Two weeks after Miraya was born, I returned to Haiti to take care of some business and ministry things as well as look after the house. At that point, she'd already gotten her birth certificate and we had applied for her passport. We had her passport in hand before she was even a month old! The hospital had told us it would be between 12 weeks to 6 months to just get her birth certificate. As soon as we had the passport in hand, we purchased plane tickets for June 11, 2018, which was much sooner than anticipated.

While the family was gone in the US, I had begun going to an English-speaking church in Petionville regularly. I began leading worship at Port-Au-Prince Fellowship once a month and then began preaching every six weeks. As I engaged in this, God began to plant a desire in me to pastor again. At first I didn't understand why God would have us go back to Haiti to then have us return, but as things unfolded, I began to understand.

We had purchased a house in Oklahoma in 2008, after I finished Officer Basic School for Field Artillery. When we moved to Haiti in 2013, we began renting the house out so that we could continue paying our mortgage on it. We had tried to sell it before going on the mission field, but he market wasn't cooperating. At this point, we were struggling with the management company who was handling the house and just wanted out from under them. Some dear friends of ours at Dayspring Community Church were having their own issues with the house they were renting. As we heard of their situation, we felt God was asking us to allow them to rent our house. Before we left in June, we had spoken with them and offered them the house. They were extremely excited. Robby and Mikalah had been in the youth group when I was the youth pastor and I had the privilege of being very involved in their lives as they grew and matured. Robby was one of the regular drummers at the church and Mikalah had become one of the worship leaders at Dayspring. What's more is that I had been a sort of father-figure for Mikalah during her high school years, so she spent a great deal of time in that very house.

Though they had not yet moved in when I started realizing God was preparing us to go back to the States, I felt I could not rescind my offer of the house. God had other plans for us and it did not involve going back to the same place from which we had come. Cathi and I talked and prayed about it a great deal. We both struggled with the idea of this change but agreed that it made sense with everything that God had done in us thus far. We also agreed that we would not start looking for a pastoral position until December of that year. I'd shared this with my accountability partners and with mentors in my life who had prayed with and for us and agreed this was in line with what God had been doing. The teaching ministry was clearly flourishing under Pastor Thenor's leadership and I was enjoying hearing how God was using him in this capacity. Additionally, the school IBC had managed to keep both the certificate and diploma programs open simultaneously, hire more staff, double their student body, and were now adding a third program with TLI's help. My reasons for joining them were no longer existing problems and it was clear I needed to step back and let them continue moving forward. As I began my third year of teaching with them, I broke the news of our pending move to the United States. Their response was humbling. They thanked me for my involvement and encouraged me in the next chapter God was writing in my life.

In August, I got a call from a friend about a position for a Missions Pastor that he'd seen posted on a church jobs site. I looked at the listing and started praying about it. Additionally, I set up a profile on the site with my resume posted and so forth. After I had done so, I started receiving calls from other churches. I even received one from the US Army Chaplaincy to recruit me. I chuckled as I knew that boat had sailed a long time ago. One of the churches that called had a position for Worship and Missions Pastor. I was intrigued since those two things were huge passions that God had not only given me, but allowed me to engage in. I looked up the job listing, saved it to my profile, then talked to Cathi about it. After we looked at it together, we decided no for several reasons to include location and size of the church. When I went to delete it from my saved listings, I saw another listing for Pastor of Worship and Connections at Kossuth Street Baptist Church in Lafayette, Indiana. Again, pairing those two positions was intriguing to me, so I clicked on it to read more about it.

The more I read and the more I researched from their website, the more I was drawn to it. It was August 20 and we weren't supposed to start looking or applying to anything until December! But I couldn't escape the desire to shoot them an e-mail and see what happened. It was the only application or resume I'd have to send. By December, I was on my way to Lafayette with Cathi and Miraya to visit the church and do an in-person interview. As we visited the church and interacted with the elders, the worship team, and others, we felt at home. It wasn't perfect, but neither are we. However, we could see God's fingerprint all over this. At the end of that visit, they announced that they wanted to move forward with me as the candidate they would present to the church.

In January, the church flew the whole family up to the church for us to experience it together. I preached one Sunday, then led worship the following Sunday. My kids had the opportunity to be involved in youth group, kids' programs, and everything that week. Cathi met with other ladies, particularly the elders' wives and begin establishing relationships with them. We were so loved and welcomed that we in turn wanted to be a part of that community. At every turn, God confirmed that this was his will for us – both the church and us as a family.

During the trip in January, we nearly froze. We had snow storms the first weekend we were there and sub-freezing temperatures the second. Isaac loved the snow, though. He couldn't truly remember it from our time living in the States, since he was so little when we moved to Haiti. He got to play in the snow to his heart's content. I don't think we did too badly in adjusting to the cold. But even better was the fact that the folks of KSBC got us clothes for the cold weather. Each of us got a jacket and gloves and a hat. They also got us sweaters and socks. I mean, they went all out and made sure we had warm clothing for the time we were there. It was very sweet.

We were so struck by God's faithfulness in it all. I knew he only wanted me to focus on that one church and not put any more applications or resumes out everywhere – which would have been my default. As a result, I was able to begin developing relationships with the elders even through the application and interview process. My kids even told me that they were not overwhelmed. In their heads, they just thought of Kossuth as the direction in which we were headed, from the beginning, because I was not dealing with multiple churches. God was so good and gentle with us. While it was sad to think of leaving Haiti, it was also exciting to see and experience God's leading and direction so clearly. When we returned from that trip on January 22, we started packing up things here and there, so that we could be ready to move by March 1st.

Little did we know our world would get turned upside down...

17 THE LAST THREE DAYS: DAY ONE

On Monday morning, February 11, 2019, I woke up at 4:30am and helped load up my sister-in-law and her family into my vehicle to take them to the airport in Port-au-Prince, Haiti. It was the start of my last three days in Haiti that would test me beyond myself and cause me to rely on God in new ways.

My family had arrived the previous Thursday, February 7 in order to help us pack and prepare to move from Haiti to the States. Additionally, my brother-in-law, Jeavon was going to help me with the last pastors' conference I was doing that Saturday, February 9. When they arrived, they announced that there would be protests as a result of many different circumstances in the country. When we moved to Haiti six years ago, the exchange rate was 40 Haitian gourdes to the American dollar. This day it was around 85 HTG to the US dollar. Money has less than half the buying power in just 6 years. And the rate of depreciation has gotten steep, since in November, the rate was more like 65 HTG to the dollar. At the same time, the rate of inflation of all goods – to include food – has skyrocketed. People can't even afford to feed their families. As if that wasn't enough, there are gas shortages every 3 weeks or so. No diesel or gasoline for vehicles or generators to provide power in a country that can't afford to give power nationwide. For these things and more, people took to protests. On Thursday, when the family came in, the streets were empty and I made it to the airport and back to the house in record time. Protests have come to be a pretty regular thing and while inconvenient, taking the proper precautions makes it still livable.

On Friday morning, the protests had intensified and I got a call from the hosting pastor to call off the conference. We tentatively rescheduled for the following Saturday. Jeavon and I spent Friday and Saturday helping some folks in the community and packing up stuff in our house. They would take back some suitcases for us to the States that we could pick up from them after our move. As things progressed Saturday, we decided it would be unsafe to make the 45-minute drive to the church we normally attend. We had received word that the bridge in Tabarre had been taken over and burning barricades were placed there. Shooting was frequent now in that area and cars were not able to make it across the bridge. This is the main bridge between our house and the city of Port-au-Prince. It was the route we took to get to church, the grocery store, the airport, and everything else!

Sunday morning we stayed at the house and continued to work. That afternoon, we went to visit our long-time friends in the nearby village of Chambrun. We hadn't been able to visit for some time, due to our travels to Indiana the previous two months. We sat and chatted for a while. Then, when the sun began to set, we started walking back. Up the road a ways, Miguel asked me if he could show Kaedon, his cousin, the voodoo tree in the center of the village. I thought it would be neat to show Jeavon, too, so the four of us took off that way while Cathi and the others continued down the road. This was the same tree that I had accidentally broken a branch off years back and incited the voodoo community's curses on me. I was intrigued as to why Miguel wanted to come here. As we approached the voodoo temple, I could see branches all over the place. It was dead wood already, but nobody had moved it. Behind the temple, where the tree once stood tall now sat a stump about my height, with the rest of the tree fallen over on its side. The branches everywhere were from this tree. Miguel pointed out the most intriguing thing was that the tree appeared to have rotted from the inside out. It was now as hollow as the spiritual power it had once stood for. Miguel had seen the tree the previous week when he went to the village to help another missionary put up trusses for a community center there.

We arrived back at the house and continued to receive reports all throughout that night that the situation on the streets was getting worse and worse. Although Jeavon and the family had tickets for a 5:30pm flight, we decided that it would be better to leave as early as possible to maximize our safety and the likelihood of arriving at the airport and me returning well. The reports from Saturday night were that the shooting went on until just after midnight. We figured at 5am we could find the calmest time for the drive. We hoped they'd be sleeping at that time.

Day One

Monday morning, we pulled out of our gate at 5am onto the empty street. The headlights pierced the pitch black as we drove away from the safety of our house. Half a mile from the house, we came up on a barricade of tires and rocks in the middle of the street. I stopped the car, looked at Jeavon. "You ready?" With a nod, we got out of the car and cleared a hole in the barricade just big enough for the SUV to get through. We worked as fast as we could and ran back to the car, jumped in and drove on. As we took the turn in the road ahead, we came up on yet another barricade. This one had more than just rocks and tires. There were tables and chairs, as well as whole market stands blocking the road. Once again, we looked at each other, nodded, and got out of the car. As soon as we'd shut the doors to the vehicles, we started hearing thudding noises - "crack!" all around us. Rocks were being hurled from the darkness at us. We quickly got back into the vehicle and I started backing up.

As I backed up, I saw two men coming into the light. One had an automatic weapon and the other a pistol. With either stupidity, desperation, or boldness (I'm not sure which), I rolled down my window and shouted, "I have kids in the car who have to get to the airport." Immediately, one of the men called for the rocks to stop being thrown. One last rock slammed into the side of the SUV, just inches from a window. The armed man yelled again for the rocks to stop, then he told me to turn the headlights off. I complied. He walked up to the window, peered into the car and then turned around to call for someone else. The one who I presume was the leader of this band of gangsters walked over and asked me where I was from. I told him I was from the community and reiterated that I had kids that needed to get out of the country. He bit his lip and shook his head. My heart now felt like it was pounding through my chest as my grip on the steering wheel tightened. The leader looked at me and said, "I'll let you through. However, know that we were ordered to set this up by others who have barricades up a mile from here and another again a mile from there. You won't find those as easy to get around." I breathed a sigh of relief and I thanked him, then quickly added, "If it's that bad, we'll turn around." He said that was probably best and helped me turn the car around so we could return to the house. On the short trip back to the house, the only sound was the sobbing of my nephew, Azar, as he cried in Kerri's arms. We pulled back into the driveway, discouraged, dismayed, and defeated. Cathi heard us pull back in and came out. Azar ran up to her and held her tight. I couldn't even begin to imagine what was going on in their minds. I encouraged everyone to try to get some sleep and we'd figure out what to do later.

I laid down, but I couldn't sleep. My heart was still pounding and my mind was going a hundred miles an hour, trying to think of what to do. I finally got up to get some coffee and breakfast. If I couldn't sleep, I needed to be as awake as possible to come up with a plan of action. I learned later that Jeavon had gone to lay down to get his emotions out and try to get focused after hearing his wife Kerri and son Azar crying. Kerri was still up, so we talked and debriefed for a while. She appeared quite shaken. We talked of calling the airline to see if we could get their flight switched to the next day or later to give us time for things to calm down. When Jeavon got up, we talked about that as an option. Cathi had gotten a message from one of our missionary friends whose Haitian husband drives a motorcycle. He suggested that he and his two brothers could get the family out on motos. Motorcycles can get through and around barricades much easier than a car. He also knows other back roads to go back and forth in order to avoid some of the major intersections where they would likely set up road blocks. He said he would hop on his moto and try to make it to our house to see what the situation was like. In the meantime, Cathi started making pancakes, trying to do something normal to lighten the mood and lift our spirits. As kids got up, they ate and resumed doing normal things.

Within an hour, Jimmy was at our house. He said they let him through that same barricade and told us where the other one was between our house and his. He was pretty confident he could get around everything and get to the airport using a bridge on the west side that he said was clear. He said he'd just gone into town the day before using that bridge and had no issues. That gave us hope. Jimmy stayed for a little bit, had breakfast with us, then took off again, saying that if we needed him we just had to call him. I sat down with Google maps open and started studying different routes that would avoid intersections. In the end, I mapped out a whole route that would get us to that bridge on the west side. In the meantime, Jeavon was on the phone with the airline to see if he could change the tickets. At one point, they told him they could confirm seats as early as the next day, but there would be some fees involved. Willing to make the change, he asked me if he should do it. I told him I thought we could make it, using the route I'd mapped out, but we would need to leave before noon. He agreed and hung up the phone. We decided to test the route before we took everyone on it. We jumped in the car and went down the road. There would be no hiding in the darkness, but there would also be no headlights to give us away. A quarter of a mile from our house, before reaching that first barricade, I turned right down an alleyway in between houses. The gravel path led us to a dirt road that followed the power lines that went into town. We'd follow those to the next major street. Halfway down the road, we passed a gentleman who motioned that he was hungry. I rolled down my window and offered him some money and asked him at the same time how the road was ahead. As he took the money with gratitude in his eyes, he said the road was clear all the way through. We thanked him and headed back to the house.

Goodbyes were said a second time as Jeavon's family piled into the SUV once again. My stomach was in knots. We followed the same route, passed the same man by the side of the road and kept going towards the main road ahead. At the paved road, we turned and went down. It was clear as far as we could see, so I gunned the engine and sped down the road. A couple of miles down, I spotted a barricade up ahead made up of tires. They were opening up for a car in front of us to get through, so I sped up and slid through behind it. I didn't stop to ask or see if they were ok with it. A short distance later, however, we came upon another and this time, the vehicle in front started turning around. I spotted an entrance to a street on the left and went down that dirt road a ways before stopping to check the map. I saw where we were and what direction we needed to go in order to get to the bridge. The road to that bridge wasn't all that far away. We started making our way down these unfamiliar back streets that crisscrossed and intertwined. I hit a couple of dead-ends that didn't show up on the map before I stopped asked someone by the side of the road how to get to the bridge. I repeated the verbiage from this morning that I had kids who had to get to the airport to leave the country. The people eagerly provided information. They actually advised us to stay away from the bridge. They said, "Don't go near it. People took control of it this morning and are throwing rocks at any car that tries to get by. You're better off going the other direction and going through the river. Do you know that crossing?" I told them I'd been through it once before, so he provided more specifics for me until he could see I was understanding and we took off again. Thankfully, these back roads were pretty calm, though the driving was slower because they were very bumpy.

I got to a place where I could get to another major road, not far from the river crossing. I turned onto that road and gunned it again to get as far as I could. Unfortunately, not far ahead, I could see burning barricades set up all across the road. But as with a previous road block, I saw some people moving rocks out of the way to let a car in front of us pass. I tried to do the same as before and sneak in after him, but I was stopped. Immediately, the car was surrounded by a dozen young men, most of them antagonizing and harassing. One of them spoke to me and asked what I was doing. I explained our situation with the kids needing to get to the airport. He said he controlled the area and was willing to send some of these men on motos to ensure our safety, but I would have to pay them on the other end. This was a gang leader and though he expressed this as an option, it was clear I didn't have a choice. It was do things his way or else. I didn't want to find out what the "else" would be.

I told him no problem and immediately two jumped on top of my vehicle, two others grabbed motos and a few others hopped on behind them. There were seven men in all serving as our "escort." They sped away on the motos and motioned for me to follow close behind. Saying a prayer under my breath, I stepped on the gas to keep up. As I followed them, I took note of the pistols I saw tucked into their pants. There was another burning barricade ahead. Before we even got to it, they motioned and people cleared a hole for us. Even further up the road, there were boulders set up in the street. This time, no hole was being made. Instead, there were nasty looks behind exchanged. As I slowed to a stop, our car was surrounded by more people than I could count in that moment. Some of them started picking up large rocks and others placed themselves directly in front of the car. Some of our escorts proceeded to get into a shouting and shoving match with these guys and eventually, we were able to push through the hostile crowd and continue driving. They made a right turn between a couple of buildings about half a mile before the road to Tabarre bridge. We turned in between the buildings and struggled to keep up with the motos as they traversed the bumpy dirt road far more easily than our SUV.

The guys riding on top continue to shout for us to keep going. I kept fearing that they would fly off the top, but somehow they managed to stay on. As I drove, I pulled my wallet out of my back pocket and gave it to Jeavon and asked him to pull out some money to give the guys. I thought there were six guys, so I told him to pull out $60. I put that money under my right thigh, put some Haitian money in my left pocket, then returned the wallet to my back pocket.

Up ahead, one of the motos was waiting where it appeared the road ended. As we pulled closer, we could see that it was a steep slope downward to the riverbed. Since the bridges were controlled by other gangs, the riverbed made sense. There was nobody down there. I braked the whole way down the embankment and drove across maybe five or six inches of water. In the middle of dry season, we hadn't had rain for weeks now, allowing for the river to be passable. On the other side, we ran alongside of the riverbank before driving up the other side. The motos still pressed faster than we could go. We ran along several back streets on that side of the river that I had never used before. The motos stopped and one of the men came up to the window. He said that just beyond that building I would be on the main road again, so I should pay him now and they would return. I gave him the $60 and said thank you. He said that it wasn't enough. He said there were seven of them, so I needed to give a little more. I reached into my left pocket and pulled out the Haitian cash and showed there was nothing else in my front pockets. He said, ok, grabbed the money and they took off. Once again, I breathed a sigh of relief.

I checked my map again to make sure I got my bearings. To our left was a major intersection – Carrefour Flerio. I figured we would inch our way out of the alley and see what that intersection looked like. I expected it to be barricaded with tires burning and everything, forcing us to go right. Instead, I saw tons of police officers on the corner, in armor and heavily armed, standing guard at the intersection. I turned toward the intersection and as we took a right towards the airport, I looked back and saw billows of smoke coming from the other side of the intersection, towards the bridge. It was as if that road we had just come down was the dividing line between the two fighting forces. The rest of the way was completely clear, as there was a large police presence. The next intersection marked the boundary of the UN base and beyond that, a police station. The airport also has another police station and as we pulled closer, we could see that there were additional security forces posted at the airport. We sang and shouted praises to God that we had made it.

We got the luggage out of the car and then we hugged fiercely. I told them I would wait here at the airport until I received word that they were checked in and confirmed on the flight. As they went inside the airport, I broke down and started crying. The weight of responsibility for their safety was too much. But God had provided and protected. Even the gangsters that were merely helping for profit were part of His provision for us. I called Cathi and told her we had arrived safely and they were on their way home. "Praise God," she said. We had an emotional conversation though I refrained from sharing too many details before I got home. She mentioned that some friends of ours that lived close to the airport had said that if they could help in any way, their doors were open. I decided to head that way and maybe sleep for a little bit before heading back.

I went back the way I came and then turned down their street. The grocery store there where we usually shopped was all closed up along with all the other businesses on that street. There was no one on this stretch of road. As I went through the next intersection, I saw another road block up ahead. They were letting someone else through, so I figured I'd state my case and see what happened. People there were asking for payment in order to pass. Though I still had some money in my wallet, I knew that I'd have to pay to get back out of here and I still didn't know what was beyond this before the house. I decided to turn around. Thankfully, there was no rock throwing here. I went back up the road to where the police were standing guard and breathed deep as I reluctantly left the safety of this area.

Since I had been following motos to this spot, I wasn't paying a lot of attention to how we had gotten there. I pulled onto the alley-like dirt road and then pulled out my phone. I traced the road to the river, but the question was where we had crossed. I prayed that I would somehow recognize it and headed in that direction. Thankfully, there was absolutely nothing on those roads and I was able to get to the edge of the river. Then, I began to follow the road along the river, trying to spot an opening to cross it. I came upon some folks at a fruit stand and asked how I could get across the river. One gentleman offered to get into the car and show me the way, since he was heading in that direction. I eagerly opened up and let him in. As he got in, I noticed he was holding a level, which seemed to indicate he was a mason. He confirmed this when he introduced himself as "Boss Eddy." The title Boss is what you call a foreman or skilled worker in Haiti. He guided me through the streets down to the riverbed, across, and up the other side. As we drove, I asked him if he was a believer. He told me that if it wasn't for God, he wouldn't be here. He proceeded to tell me of an accident he had the year before in which he almost died. He gave God credit for his survival and recovery. He said he likes to help people because God helped him. Once again, God's provision in the timeliest way. We came up on the road controlled by the moto gang and he told me to jog over to the dirt road across the street. As we crossed, I could see barricades a quarter mile in either direction, but not here. On the other side, he shook my hand and said I could let him off there and wished me well on the rest of the trip. I thanked him profusely.

As I pulled away, I realized that I knew where I was. I pulled out my phone to confirm and mapped a route back home, staying on these side roads. I put the phone away and continued towards the house, continuing to pray and sing the whole way. About a mile away from the house, I called Cathi and told her I would be home soon, in tears once again. As I pulled up to the house, my kids opened the gate for me. I sat in the car, tears streaming down my face as I thanked God for being with us in such a clear way that day. Then, I went inside to tell Cathi I believed it was time for us to consider getting out ourselves. We decided we would sleep on it and not make any hasty decisions.

One of the things that Jeavon and Kerri helped us to do was to pack up 13 additional bags to give to another group that was leaving Haiti on Tuesday. The group's leaders were former missionaries in Haiti and friends of ours. We hosted a Thursday night Bible study that they were part of, so we had gotten to know them well. They came on Friday night of the last week to drop off some suitcases that we could fill up for them. They had come to Haiti with supplies, which meant they had the ability to carry things back. An extra 13 checked bags is nothing short of a huge blessing, so we were excited. The caveat was that I had to get the bags to the airport on Tuesday at 11am so that they could take them. Monday night, I got a message from them saying that they would be leaving at 7am and would be under police escort to the airport. We would caravan on the way there. It seemed like a good plan, but I still didn't feel good about it – or the fact that I had to make another trip to the airport!

18 THE LAST THREE DAYS: DAY TWO

I woke up and had coffee and an apple. I couldn't stomach much more than that with the nerves I had. Unfortunately, the night had not provided much sleep as I tossed and turned, replaying scenes from the previous day in mind over and over again. All night, my heart pounded in my chest and in my head. In the morning, I asked our night time security guard, Easy, if he would be willing to ride with me to the airport and he agreed. I told him we would leave at daybreak, which would be around 6:15am. I planned to use the same route I had used the day before to get to the team's guesthouse, which was on our side of the bridge and also very close to it.

At 6:15 we set out. I turned onto the back roads just beyond our house and stuck to them all the way to their house. Everything was very quiet. It was unnerving, because of everything else going on. But I was grateful to have an uneventful ride there, so we arrived with twenty minutes to spare. I greeted the team and was briefed on the plan. There were three vehicles – all the same Mitsubishi Montero DID. Two would have the team members and the third was mine, with all the luggage. They had hired three police officers who were going to come and accompany us to the airport. One would drive one of the vehicles, but the other two would drive motos in front of the convoy, much like the gangsters had done for us yesterday.

As 7am came and went, we all got a bit nervous and unsettled. They had not yet arrived. The reason for leaving at 7am was to try to stay ahead of the severe protesting, which usually ramps up as the day goes on. The earlier, the less intense things tend to be. Leaving later would be to forfeit that advantage. Mike, the group leader, kept calling his contact who assured him that they were coming. Finally, at 7:45, they arrived and we learned the reason for their delay was that they were scouting the route before taking us on it. They were in plain clothes, but armed. I talked with one of them of the route that I had used the day before with no issues. He seemed to think it was a good idea and went to discuss with the others of the group. Meanwhile, we huddled up and prayed fervently for safety and for peace. Without delay, we all piled into the vehicles and started off. They put me as the lead vehicle, just behind the motos. We took to the back roads and crossed the main road heading for the riverbed. However, we didn't continue heading for the riverbed. The motos kept bearing left and eventually dumped out on the main road, just before the bridge! My heart sank.

I had no choice but to follow. The rest of the team was behind and if I turned around, I risked everyone's safety. My vehicle edged out onto the bridge and just like the day before, we were immediately swarmed by gangsters. The cops on the motos grabbed their attention and I could see an exchange of money being made right there. The gangster who received the money yelled for the others to back off. Our safety had been purchased. They walked alongside our vehicle and opened up paths for us to take through the multiple barricades that were set up on the bridge. There were people yelling and screaming all around us, broken glass all over the road, and tons of debris from rocks and boulders. But we were escorted straight through to the other side. I couldn't help but think of Psalm 23, "Yay though I walk through the valley of the shadow of death, I will fear no evil, for you are with me."

On the other side, past the last barricade, we gunned the engines and took to the back roads on the right. The road in front had more barricades being set up as we watched. The road was narrow with buildings on either side of the street between the bridge and the next intersection where I had seen the cops the day before. It was too big of a risk and bottleneck. These roads paralleled the roads I had taken the day before. In fact, they dumped out at the exact same spot the gangsters yesterday had left me. As we piled onto the street and headed to the protected intersection, I noticed there were remnants of rocks and debris from a barricade that we drove through. At the guarded intersection, we sped down the road once again through the protected streets to the airport.

At the airport, we offloaded the luggage and got the team inside to check in. Mike told me that he had asked at least one of the police officers to accompany me back to the guest house. The two on motos were already gone, so I figured the officer who had driven one of the other vehicles would come with me. I spotted him and he made for the driver's seat, so I gave him the keys to my car. I hopped in and we were off again just as quickly as we had arrived. As we approached the intersection with the heavily armed police, we saw that the road beyond had multiple barricades and some were already lit. To the right, which was the road that led to the US Embassy, there were more barricades in the distance. The only option was the way we had come. As we headed down that back road, the officer asked me about the river crossing. This was the same policeman that I had spoken to before we had left. Apparently, he hadn't been fond of crossing over the bridge either. I pointed out which way to go and he went. Before long, we reached the guest house, where he had left his motorcycle. I thanked him and we parted ways. I made the same route that I had the day before and made it home safely once again. I had made it to the airport and back two days in a row. There was no denying God's grace in that.

As I went inside the house, I thanked Easy for accompanying me. Then I found Cathi and embraced her. She told me she had already spoken to the kids about packing up because we were going to leave as soon as we had the opportunity. I tried to get on the phone with the airline to change our tickets, but couldn't hold a call with the faulty cell reception. I could make VOIP calls, but the airline had such a long wait/hold time, that the call would drop before I could talk to a representative. Instead, I got a message out to the former pastor from our sending church and we spoke on the phone.

I explained the situation and gave him our flight and credit card information. About 30 minutes later, as he was on hold, he texted me asking me if I still wanted to change the flight, since we were going to be charged over $2,000 in fees to change it. It was $200 per ticket, plus the change in price per ticket. I texted back a quick yes and 30 minutes later it was a done deal. He told me we were leaving the next day at 1:40pm.

Now the pressing issue was to get packed up to be ready to go. We had already begun the process of selling some of our things in Haiti, so that we could purchase them again in the States when we arrived. Some things had sold and were waiting to be picked up. Due to the unrest, nobody was coming out to us to pick anything up – and understandably so. At this point, I was thinking we just needed to pack our essentials and cut our losses. Our vehicle alone represented $15,000 that would go towards another vehicle for us in the States, but I was ready to drive it to the airport and abandon it so that we could get out. Cathi then told me that the folks at Nehemiah Vision Ministries – the organization we worked for our first three years Haiti – were coming over soon to help us with the packing. More than that, they were also considering leaving. An hour later, the seven members of the American staff at NVM came to the house with a flat bed truck to help us pack and haul stuff to their ministry campus and put our things into a container there for storage. We were overwhelmed with this display of love and grace.

It was now about 11 o'clock in the morning and we began working, room by room to pack what we were taking with us and what was going to NVM for storage. Matt and I started taking apart beds and putting them on his truck, hauling dressers, and the bigger pieces. We'd drive the two miles down to the campus and put them into an empty container. On the trip to the campus, we saw the remnants of a burned barricade on the road. Our area, which was normally very peaceful, was showing the signs of the riots and protests too. More and more, the signs pointed to something else. This was no longer just a discontented people, but a show of force to take over the country. What started as protests had become an attempted coup. We had heard the news that the opposition was threatening to keep this up until the president stepped down. The words spoken were that they would burn Haiti to the ground if he did not resign. They were living up to their words. Normally during protests, there are times of reprieve given to allow people to re-stock on food and drinking water and gas for those who had vehicles or generators. But no such reprieve was being given. Instead, they pushed on more and more intensely each day. Gas stations were being looted, banks burned down. There was no end in sight. We had enough diesel for two more nights of generator use and enough food to last until the end of the week. But after that, there were no stores to get anything from or gas stations to get fuel, as they were not being restocked either. The strategy seemed to be a siege on the capital city.

As the ladies packed up more and more stuff, we made multiple trips in order to empty the house. I stopped at one point to eat a sandwich, recognizing that I'd barely eaten in the last 24 hours. I was running on pure adrenaline. During one of the loading trips, some of the missionaries were getting online with my hotspot in order to book tickets out. They all got onto the same flight, so that we could all make the trip to the airport together. Once again, God was providing. We wouldn't need to drive our vehicle and abandon it. Additionally, we would spend the night at NVM before heading out with everyone in the morning.

Around 5pm, the NVM crew called it a night and went back to campus. We stayed to finish packing up our stuff to take. There were still some major items that hadn't made it to NVM, but Matt and Megan said they would return the next day to take care of them. They had decided to stay in Haiti along with Brooke, one of the NVM nurses. We took the next couple of hours to pack up our room, which we had left for last. I had the mentality of leaving whatever behind, while Cathi was ensuring we had what we needed. It was a good balance. I was striving for speed, while she was trying to set us up well. In the end, we did end up leaving some things that we probably should have brought with us, but nothing that we could not live without. During this time, I started hearing people in the community getting rather riled up and I was hoping to get out of the house and to NVM as soon as possible. Earlier in the day there were two tires across the street from the house and I was beginning to think they were setting up a road block right in front of the house. I wasn't excited about what that would mean for us trying to get out of the house.

At 8pm, we piled up the rest of our bags in our car with us and left the house for the last time. Thankfully, there was no barricade outside the house. But I couldn't believe that we had literally packed up the whole house in less than 12 hours. If it hadn't been for the NVM staff, that would not have been possible. As we pulled onto the NVM campus, we were so grateful for them and their help. Matt and Megan had grabbed our food from the fridge at our house and were cooking some of that for us to eat for dinner. Brooke had set up an intern house for us to use that night to sleep. We ate in a more lighthearted mood, then the kids headed over to the children's home on campus to say goodbye to some friends. I went to find Adam, the Missions Director to get the scoop on our plan for the morning. He said we'd be loading up the vehicle at 9pm. That wasn't too long from then, so I went to the team center where they were bringing the vehicle. Earlier in the day, Adam had said that a bus was likely and he was asking about the route that I used to get to the airport. I told him I didn't think that the bus would make it through the river crossing because of the steep river banks in and out. Adam soon came over and said we were going to take an ambulance.

Someone had donated an ambulance to NVM several years before to use in their Medical Center. Since that center wasn't fully operational, they often took the ambulance to do mobile medical clinics so that they had a space in which to do private screenings. I don't think it's even licensed for use in Haiti, but I suppose that wasn't a factor at this point. Adam said that the ambulance had been overheating a few days prior, so the mechanics had worked on it and took it for a test run. The thought process was that people might be more likely to let an ambulance through. But also, since the back was all covered, we'd be safer if people decided to start throwing rocks. Because of its size, we also couldn't take the ambulance down the back road or the river crossing, so it meant we would have to take the main road all the way – even across the bridge. The ambulance made its way over and Clerice got out. I found out he would be driving us in the morning. He and two other Haitians – one a doctor and the other an engineer – would ride up front to get us to the airport. Clerice is a dear friend of mine. I was the best man in his wedding several years ago and my kids know him as Tonton (Uncle) Clerice. He has been a major part of our lives since our arrival in Haiti. If we encountered any problems, he would be in great danger as the driver of the vehicle.

When I worked at Nehemiah Vision Ministries, I served as the Missions Director. Three years in, NVM hired Adam and I trained him to be my replacement there. Before going to serve in Haiti, Adam was a paramedic for a fire department. He had much experience around an ambulance, so he had all sorts of ideas where we could put bags and maximize the space available. It was quite helpful. We started putting bags in all sorts of compartments and arranging them in such a way that we would all fit just fine in the back. The group leaving in the morning would consist of my family of 7, his family of 4, and 3 other ladies for a total of 14 people. My theory was that there were two ways to make this trip: quiet and stealthy or loud and fast. We were definitely going with the latter, lights and sirens blaring down the main street. It was gutsy, but it was worth a shot. The plan was to leave at 5am. After packing up the ambulance with our luggage, we said a prayer and then went off to get some much-needed sleep before our early departure. Interestingly enough, with as much as was at stake with this operation, I had peace. That doesn't mean I wasn't nervous. But I knew God would prove Himself faithful to us, whatever that looked like. I actually slept four hours that night, which was the most I'd slept in the previous two nights.

19 THE LAST THREE DAYS: DAY THREE

That night, the generator was shut off at 1am in order to conserve power. NVM was working on conserving the diesel they still had, so they were putting generator shut-offs into effect. Thankfully, the air was cool, so we opened the windows in the intern house and stayed comfortable. At 4am, Aya woke up to nurse fifteen minutes before my alarm went off. Cathi got up to get her and I made my way to the restroom. I could hear the generator struggling to turn over. They were turning it on so that we had lights to prepare for our departure and then would turn it off after we left. It eventually kicked on and the team center lit up. People started moving about, getting ready to go.

As we got closer to 5am, we gathered by the ambulance. Matt, Megan, and Brooke were there to see us off. We circled up and prayed for the journey, for those that were staying behind, and for Haiti in general. We said and hugged goodbye. Then, we piled into the back of the ambulance. The kids were on the floor near the cab and adults surrounded, some on the seats and some of us standing. Adam and I stood in the back by the door. We kept the lights off in the back so that nobody could see inside. Clerice and one of the doctors of NVM got into the front. Philippe got into the back with us. Just as soon as we had gotten settled, we took off. The guard opened the front gate and we started down the mile-long dirt road. We bumped and jostled along that road in almost complete silence. Adam turned on the music player on his phone and it began playing the song, "Reckless Love." The only other sound was that of my daughter, Kayla, sobbing as we pulled away from our home of six years.

One mile later, we turned onto the main road and picked up speed. One more mile down this road, we stopped in front of our house. That morning, I realized that I had not grabbed my wallet with my debit card and US driver's license. I had asked Clerice if he would briefly stop there so that I could get it. As soon as the ambulance stopped, I shot out the back and tried to open the gate. It was latched shut from the inside. Not wanting to make too much noise or make a scene, I climbed up the front gate and jumped into the yard. I ran to the house and opened the front door, ran inside and to my bedroom. The door was locked. I didn't even think twice and I started to slam my shoulder into it to break it down. I knew time was limited and I didn't want to take too long. I heard Easy's voice from inside call out. So, I waited for him to open the door and quickly explained why I was back. Easy was holed up in the room to guard the last of our stuff that we hadn't been able to grab and to protect himself as well. I grabbed my wallet, hugged Easy goodbye, then rushed back outside to the ambulance.

Climbing in, I sat on top of one of my military duffel bags near the kids on the floor and in front of Cathi and the baby who were sitting on the ledge to my right. I began to pray for them, that they would not be afraid, and that God would guard their hearts. Some of the kids were talking about Star Wars and other random everyday things. From time to time their voices would get louder and an adult would "shhh" to quiet them down again. We were depending on no one knowing we were in the back. While we didn't want to dampen their spirits, we also wanted to make sure we weren't given away by their noise. I looked over at Aya who was in an infant carrier strapped to Cathi. Aya was fast asleep again and I prayed she would stay that way and not wake up. Adam asked for someone to turn the air on in the back, as it was getting quite stuffy with that many people back there. The air kicked on and we could immediately feel the difference.

We drove down the street and past the half-mile mark beyond our house. No barricade. There was a bit of debris in the road, but it was completely passable. Being in the back of the ambulance, we couldn't see anything in front. We could only see through the back windows what we had just passed on the road. I would occasionally pull out my phone, open Google maps, and follow the blue dot to see where we were. My previous two trips were on back roads, so I had no idea what to expect on this trip. However, I was pretty certain of a few problematic spots on the way to the bridge. The ambulance started slowing down and then we felt the rocking as if we were going over uneven speed bumps and then we took off again. As we passed the road block, we could see that there were no people there and that it was a relatively simply barricade of rocks across the width of the road. A glance at Google maps told me we were just beyond the intersection at Beudet, which was three and a half miles from NVM and still seven miles to the airport. We went another one and a half miles down the road before we hit the next intersection. We drove through several spots where there had clearly been barricades but had since been taken down and cleared. There was still some debris in the road. We continued that way through the intersection at Croix des Bouquets and through Route 8, which ran straight through to the Dominican Republic. We were taking it the other way towards the intersection at Marassa, just before the bridge.

As we approached the intersection, the ambulance slowed and then crawled to a stop. We heard the doors open in front and then the sounds of thudding rocks on the road as we could only picture our friends moving rocks from the road block so that we could pass. After a few short minutes, they climbed back in and we heard the doors slam shut again. The sound and slight rock of the vehicle indicated they had changed gears. The ambulance started going in reverse to the right and stopped again to change gears. Clerice put the ambulance in drive and then nothing. The engine had just died. We started praying. We heard the engine turning over as he tried to get it started again. Adam told Abby to turn off the air in the back. She did so and shortly thereafter, the ambulance roared to life again. Several people muttered a "thank you, Jesus" as we began to move again. The ambulance turned left and through the windows, I could see that we were being waved on by men manning the barricade. They were rerouting us around the barricade through an alley on the left of the street. Thank God for his favor.

Kids had started getting restless and some were trying to stand up to see out the windows, so we asked them to sit down and remain quiet. Now that we were seeing people out and about, stress and tension rose. I looked back over at Cathi and could see that Aya was still sleeping. She was sweaty, but still sleeping. As we came out of the alley and got back on the main road, the ambulance sped ahead. There were some more barricades that the ambulance drove over and through in the next quarter of a mile or so. At that point, we went around a curve in the road which put us on a straight shot towards the bridge. At this point, I began praying fervently to the extent that I did not pay much attention to what was going on outside the ambulance. The next thing that I remember was looking out the back window and seeing that we had just cleared past the bridge. Shortly thereafter, as I continued to pray, Adam asked me, "Was that there yesterday?" as he looked out the back window. I couldn't see what he was referring to, so Cathi told me there was a shipping container across the street, blocking all but the tiny opening we had fit through. Things had definitely escalated even more.

I lost count of how many times the ambulance stopped for the guys to get out and clear debris and rocks from the road to make a hole for us to pass through. Cathi said it was at least a dozen times. I also lost count of how many times the engine on the vehicle died and had to be restarted. Each time, we did not know if it would start up again. During one of those times, I smelled coolant and realized the ambulance was overheating. It was not meant to carry this much weight and maneuver like this. It was struggling. We turned off the air in the back and just resolved to be sweaty for the rest of the drive. Now that we were beyond the bridge, we were in the corridor with narrow streets and taller buildings. The street was so narrow that within the last few months, the government had issued a mandate that all buildings had to be within a certain distance away from the street. I believe it was 5 meters away. Those that were closer had to tear down all the way to 5 meters, so that the government could come in and widen the road. For the last couple of months, people had been taking sledge hammers to the fronts of homes and businesses all along that corridor in order to clear it. That meant there was plenty of debris – cement, cinder blocks, rebar – to use in making barricades there. Time and time again, our three Haitian friends stopped the ambulance to get out and clear these road blocks enough to pass. Some had tires burning, some were just rocks and boulders.

On one of these road blocks, the ambulance struggled to get over the blocks. Though they had cleared quite a bit of the blocks and cement, the boulders and rocks were big and tough to move. Clerice gunned the engine. As the ambulance lurched forward, we heard the distinct sound of a tire popping. The ambulance continued on and it became obvious that the front right tire was now flat and we were riding on the rim. The rim was grinding badly as we rolled down the street. At the next barricade, the guys went through the same process of getting out and clearing some of the road block before jumping back in. However, they were out of the ambulance a bit longer than usual. This time, only Clerice got back in to drive. The vehicle cleared the front tires over the barricade and then got stuck. Clerice tried to back it up and force it forward, but it was not getting over the road block. I looked outside as I noticed it was beginning to be light out. It must have been just after 6am. We'd been on the road for more than an hour and we hadn't even gone more than 8 miles. As I was noticing the brightening sky, I caught a glimpse of silhouettes on the roof tops around us. Looking closer, I saw they were wielding firearms. Being stuck on a barricade in between these buildings, we were an easy target. There was no way out, no escape, no hiding. They clearly saw us. I whispered, "God, help us." Kayla, sitting next to Cathi, began to turn around to look out the window. I grabbed her hand and told her to focus on what was going on inside the ambulance and not to look outside. In my mind, I thought, I don't want her to see what's coming. Even though the armed men saw us, they did nothing. If anything, they stepped back. What I didn't know then but found out later was that at that same moment, we had come into view of the intersection where the police officers were holding the line. Pastor Pierre, founder of Nehemiah Vision Ministries was also standing on that corner with them, waiting for the ambulance carrying his staff members. When he saw the ambulance, he said to the officers, "My people are in there." Though the police officers were under orders to hold the intersection and not cross to the other side, they moved forward, weapons trained on the roof tops, and surrounded the ambulance. They remained with the ambulance as it finally broke free of the barricade and continued to move towards the safety of the intersection. Two road blocks later, we rolled across the intersection. The ambulance stopped and Pastor Pierre opened the back to tell us we were now safe. With the back open, we could see the corridor we had just traversed. It was nothing short of a miracle that we had made it. As we continued to slowly drive the last couple of miles to the airport, I took the opportunity to talk to the kids sitting on the floor about God's love and protection. I don't remember my exact words, but I did tell them that they have a unique story to share of how good our God is.

As we pulled under the awning of the airport's entrance, there was laughter, smiling, and joy. It was as if you could taste the joy. All of us took turns thanking the men who had risked their lives for us by driving this vehicle. Then we started the task of unloading all those bags from the back of the ambulance to get them into the airport. Though there were tons of people at all of the check-in lines and the security check-point, it didn't matter. God had been gracious, kind, and powerful as he protected us that morning.

EPILOGUE

As we sat waiting for hours in the airport before our flight, I had the opportunity to check my e-mail and social media to see the responses to our requests for prayer. There were so many who had joined with us during that very hour we were driving to the airport and were praying for our safe passage. Our sending church in Oklahoma had people praying. Our new church home in Indiana had people praying. Ezra Vision Ministries had sent out an e-mail calling for their staff to pray for us. Our friends and family throughout the US had groups of people who were praying for us that morning. One of Cathi's sisters said that she woke up at 5:45, sensing that she needed to pray for us. That was around the time we would have cleared the bridge and started going into the deadly corridor. The unmanned barricades at the beginning of our journey were proof of God's grace, considering that just two days prior, I had rocks thrown at me at 5am. The fact that Aya slept the whole way was nothing short of a miracle. Having an ambulance that is designed to keep rolling even on flat tires was God's provision for our needs. The police officers' intervention was God's sovereign protection over us. The NVM staff coming over to help us pack the day before; not having to abandon our vehicle; making three successful trips to the airport in three days under those conditions… over and over again, we saw the grace of God as he met our every need. This was not the way we had planned – or wanted – to leave Haiti. But I pray that God is glorified in what happened as people hear our story…

As I wrote and pieced this together, not even a week had gone by since we left Haiti. The three friends who originally stayed behind – Brooke, Matt, and Megan – were evacuated as well. The day after we arrived in the States, the State Department raised the Travel Warning to Level 4, which prompted many ministries in Haiti to enforce mandatory evacuation for all of its foreign staff members. There have been others of our friends who have also evacuated, while others have still chosen to remain due to their roles and their involvement in their communities. There are parts of Haiti that have gone back to seemingly normal conditions one day and go back to protests the next. Some mornings thing seem fine only to erupt later in the day. Things are just unpredictable. We have continued to pray for peace in Haiti, for our friends and colleagues still there, and our Haitian friends that had no choice but to stay. We've been overwhelmed by the amount of those Haitians that said, without exception, that they were glad we were able to get out when we did.

Additionally, I have to remind myself that the power, grace, and provision of God we experienced so richly in the last week is nothing new. He has been moving in those ways all along. Our whole missions journey has been evidence of all of those things and more. God is faithful. He always has been and always will be.

It was therapeutic for me to write down the experience and remember what God has done for me and my family. I know it will still take more time to process it all. But the reality is that we can't deny how God's hand was over us during that whole time. We can't deny his provision in our time of greatest need. We can't deny his grace which carried us through. We can't deny God was with us.

> "For we do not want you to be unaware, brothers, of the affliction we experienced in Asia. For we were so utterly burdened beyond our strength that we despaired of life itself. Indeed, we felt that we had received the sentence of death. But that was to make us rely not on ourselves but on God who raises the dead. He delivered us from such a deadly peril, and he will deliver us. On him we have set our hope that he will deliver us again. You also must help us by prayer, so that many will give thanks on our behalf for the blessing granted us through the prayers of many."

2 Corinthians 1:8-11

ABOUT THE AUTHORS

Gami and Cathi are best friends, ministry partners, and married since 2001. God has given them five wonderful children – Miguel, Kayla, Sandra, Isaac, and Aya. Gami earned a Master of Divinity in Missional Studies from Liberty University Baptist Theological Seminary and Cathi a BS in Nutrition Science from Kaplan University. They served as missionaries to rural Haiti from 2013 to 2019, when they evacuated due to violence and political unrest. Currently, they are transitioning from their ministry in Haiti to Lafayette, Indiana, where Gami will serve as the Pastor of Worship and Connections at Kossuth Street Baptist Church.

Made in the USA
Middletown, DE
07 October 2022